עת לבכות

A
TIME
TO
WEEP

The Fall of Jerusalem and Beitar

עת לבכות

A Time to Weep

The Fall of Jerusalem and Beitar

RABBI LEIBEL RESNICK

CIS
P·U·B·L·I·S·H·E·R·S
New York · London · Jerusalem

Published and distributed
in the U.S., Canada and overseas by
C.I.S. Publishers and Distributors
180 Park Avenue, Lakewood, New Jersey 08701
(908) 905-3000 Fax: (908) 367-6666

Distributed in Israel by
C.I.S. International (Israel)
Rechov Mishkalov 18
Har Nof, Jerusalem
Tel: 02-518-935

Distributed in the U.K. and Europe by
C.I.S. International (U.K.)
89 Craven Park Road
London N15 6AH, England
Tel: 81-809-3723

Book and cover design: Deenee Cohen
Typography: Nechamie Miller

ISBN 1-56062-211-3 hard cover
1-56062-212-1 soft cover
Library of Congress Catalog Card Number
93-72409

PRINTED IN THE UNITED STATES OF AMERICA

TABLE OF CONTENTS

INTRODUCTION *13*

HISTORICAL BACKGROUND *19*

CHAPTER ONE: THE ENEMY WITHIN
Kamtza and Bar Kamtza, 66 c.e. *23*
Emperor Nero, 67 c.e. *26*
The Zealots, 68 c.e. *28*
Pangs of Hunger, 69 c.e. *32*

CHAPTER TWO: THE BATTLE FOR JERUSALEM
Titus, Nissan, 70 c.e. *49*
First Wall Breached, 7 Iyar, 70 c.e. *57*
Second Wall Breached, 12 Iyar, 70 c.e. *60*
Northern City Invaded, 17 Iyar, 70 c.e. *62*
Famine and Defection, 21 Iyar, 70 c.e. *63*
The Rampworks Collapse, 29 Iyar, 70 c.e. *68*
The Zealots Attack, 2 Sivan, 70 c.e. *69*

CHAPTER THREE: THE SIEGE OF JERUSALEM

The Siege Begins, 3 Sivan, 70 c.e. 71

Scenes of Depravity, 6 Sivan, 70 c.e. 72

Two Martyrs, 25 Sivan, 70 c.e. 74

Assault on the Antonia Fortress, 1 Tammuz, 70 c.e. 76

Antonia Captured, 5 Tammuz, 70 c.e. 77

CHAPTER FOUR: THE BATTLE FOR THE TEMPLE

Titus Offers Peace, 17 Tammuz, 70 c.e. 79

Fighting in the Temple, 22 Tammuz, c.e. 80

Temple Portico Ablaze, 24 Tammuz, 70 c.e. 82

Compassionate Mother, 27 Tammuz, 70 c.e. 84

The Wall Still Stands, 2 Av, 70 c.e. 87

The Temple Gates Burned, 8 Av, 70 c.e. 88

The Temple Captured, 9 Av, 70 c.e. 89

Woe to Me, 10 Av, 70 c.e. 92

CHAPTER FIVE: JERUSALEM IN RUINS

Gladness into Mourning, 15 Av, 70 c.e. 95

Tower of David, 16 Av, 70 c.e. 97

Retreat into the Sewers, 17 Av, 70 c.e. 99

Surrender at Last, 20 Av, 70 c.e. 101

Roman Flag in the Fortress of David, 7 Elul, 70 c.e. .. 102

Death in the Temple Courtyard, 8 Elul, 70 c.e. 103

CHAPTER SIX: AFTERMATH

Jerusalem in Ruins, 70 c.e. 105

Triumphal Parade 107

Rabban Yochanan ben Zakkai-the Light of Israel 108

Masada and the End of the First Revolt, 73 c.e. 109

Roman Rule Continues, 75-81 c.e. *115*
Nerva Rules after Domitian is Assassinated, 85-98 c.e. *118*

CHAPTER SEVEN: THE SECOND REVOLT
Trajan Seeks Revenge, 99 c.e. *121*
Hadrian Seeks to Appease Jews, 117 c.e. *125*
The Great Persecution *128*

CHAPTER EIGHT: THE THIRD REVOLT
Star of Jacob, 125 c.e. *135*
Rabbi Akiva's Rise to Greatness *139*
The Last Refuge, 132 c.e. *146*
Massacre at Betar *149*

APPENDIX: FROM THE MIDRASH
Midrashic Account of the Ten Martyrs *153*
Midrashic Account of Kamtza and Bar Kamtza *171*

GLOSSARY OF HISTORICAL PLACES AND PERSONS *179*
GLOSSARY *187*

INTRODUCTION

The Diaspora, the scattering of the Jews among the nations of the world, is the link in the chain of Jewish history that joins our illustrious past with mankind's destiny. For almost two thousand years, the Jews have wandered from land to land, sharing their ethics, ideals and talents with the nations of the world. Jews brought to their host nations not only financial success, political acumen and professional standards, but also sanctity and holiness. For this very reason, the divine edict of *galus* had been decreed. The fiery wrath of divine retribution is seen not as a punishment but as a cleansing and purification process for the Jews and the nations. The civilized world, as we know it today, is a result of the impact of the Diaspora.

We tend to think that the Diaspora began the day the Holy Temple was destroyed, but in reality, *galus* did not begin with a single moment in time. Its genesis was over the course of many years, beginning in Jerusalem with the First

Revolt against Rome and ending in the city of Betar with the fall of the messianic king, Bar Kokhba. The Genesis of the Diaspora spanned a period of approximately seventy years. From the viewpoint of modern historians, this seventy-year period is divided into two eras: before Josephus and after Josephus.

Josephus Flavius was a Jewish historian who lived through the destruction of the Second Temple. In his younger years, he served as a Temple priest and later became a general of the Judean troops in the Galilee during the First Revolt against Rome. Josephus realized the futility of the war and surrendered to the Romans. He became a pacifist and firmly believed that the Jews would be granted a good deal of autonomy and self-determination if they would discontinue the revolt and surrender. The Jews would be able to conduct their religious and political affairs as they had been doing until the Judean rebellion against Rome. Many of the Jewish sages shared this view.

Josephus accompanied the Roman troops through the Galilee and eventually southward into Jerusalem. Throughout the war, he urged his fellow countrymen to surrender, but his pleas fell on deaf ears. Josephus sensed the tragedy that was about to befall his beloved nation, and he faithfully recorded his observations and analysis of the unfolding events.

When the war was over and the Holy City was in ruins, he wrote a detailed account of those events. The book was written in Aramaic and is known as *Sefer Yossifon*. It was later translated into Hebrew. Josephus subsequently wrote another two volumes in Greek, the universal language of the times. The first volume was a history of the Jewish people called *Antiquities of the Jews*. The second volume was called *Wars of the Jews*. It detailed the events and wars of the era, beginning with the Maccabean revolt, two hundred years prior to the destruction of the Temple, and concluding with the Roman victory celebration in Rome.

The sincerity and virtue of Josephus have always been called into question. Even the authenticity and accuracy of his writings have been doubted. This criticism did not originate with Jewish scholars. It was the Christian Church who first cast doubt on Josephus' reliability. Josephus had recorded every detail that affected Jewish political and religious life during the first century of the Common Era, yet he made no mention of the Christian messiah. How could the church scholars not question Josephus' works? Many Christian historians branded Josephus as a liar and scoundrel, claiming that his words were the results of his fertile imagination and twisted mind. Many Jews were duped by the initiative of the Church and began to doubt the validity of Josephus' writings.

In defense of Josephus, it is sufficient to say that our greatest and most venerated Jewish scholars did not have this doubt. Rashi quotes Josephus twenty-one times in *Tanach* and the Talmud.

Other rabbinical commentators who used and referred to Josephus include Rabbeinu Sadya Gaon, Rabbeinu Gershom, *Sefer Aruch*, Rashbam, Tosfos (*Avoda Zarah* 10b), Raavad, Baal HaMeor, Ibn Ezra, Radak, Ramban (Genesis 49:31 and *Gittin* 36a), Abarbanel, Maharal of Prague, Bach and Tosfos Yom Tov, among others.

Modern archeological discoveries have also borne out the accuracy of Josephus' descriptions. The discovery and subsequent excavations of Masada have verified Josephus' accounts to the minutest detail.

Josephus has in fact made an accurate and invaluable contribution to the history of the Jews. His eyewitness accounts of the Roman invasion, the destruction of the Holy Temple and the fall of Masada present a soul-stirring and sobering chronicle of that dark period.

A Time to Weep: The Fall of Jerusalem and Betar, the first part of this work, begins with the Roman march on Jerusalem and continues with the destruction of the Temple and the downfall of Masada. It has been based extensively on the works of Josephus, and it conveys his emotional and political views. It has also been supplemented with the Midrashic writings of our Sages.

The second part of this work deals with the Second and Third Jewish uprisings, the Great Persecution, Betar, the Ten Martyrs and Bar Kokhba. Unfortunately, there are no reliable historical records for this epoch of hope and horror; Josephus had died. There was only one Roman historian who made any effort to capture this time period for posterity, Dio Cassius. Dio Cassius was born thirty years after the city of Betar had fallen, so, unlike the works of Josephus Flavius, we do not have a firsthand account of the events. Most of Dio Cassius' works have been lost, and only a few extracts remain. Concerning the Bar Kokhba and Betar time period, there are a few brief paragraphs. There is no mention of Bar Kokhba by name or any mention of the city of Betar.

There are a score or so of Talmudic and Midrashic references to this period. However, these sources present several difficulties.

1) Often the word "emperor" is employed without any specific name attached. There were six emperors during these sixty-five years. If the proper name is not given, it is very difficult to determine to which specific reign the Midrashic incident refers.

2) The Talmud and Midrash use the term "emperor" to refer to any government administrator who was acting in an official capacity. Whether the recorded story involved the emperor himself or some other political figure cannot usually be determined.

3) The Talmud and Midrash use hyperbolic description and symbolic language to describe an event. It cannot always be determined whether the incident happened exactly as told or not.

What can be determined from these sources is the spirit of the times and how our Sages viewed and interpreted the events.

Almost every detail of the chronology of those years has been debated in modern times by religious and secular historians. I have made little attempt to assume the guise of final arbitrator in these matters. Rather, it is my view that history is a story that portrays the emotions of the times. Its chronology and facts may not always be accurate, not because of intentional deception or poor research, but because the truth cannot always be determined. The historian must take an educated guess in order to reconstruct what actually occurred.

With this in mind, I have written an account of these years with the primary goal of presenting the spirit of the times. The hopes and disappointments of the Jews, their triumphs and tragedies, the mood and climate are more vital to the surviving generations than to know exact names and dates with any degree of certainty. However, I have tried to the best of my limited ability to be rigorous in the pursuit of historical accuracy.

Recent archeological findings in the Holy Land have shed some light on this obscure era. The discoveries enable us to form images in our minds of the physical structures and battlegrounds referred to in the text. These insights have also been incorporated into this book.

As you read through this book, you will find that the distinction between friend and foe becomes blurred by the clouds of battle. We begin to cheer for the Jews, pretending we do not know the dreadful outcome, as though our hopes could change the course of history. When the war comes to its brutal climax, our hopes are dashed. We see the tragedy in our mind's eye and feel the devastation in our hearts.

"Those who mourn for Jerusalem will merit to see her rejoicing." (*Taanis* 30a)

"May it be said that the days of mourning are over so we may go forth in His light." *Kinos Arzei Halevanon*

L.R.
Sivan, 5753 (1993)
Monsey, N.Y.

HISTORICAL BACKGROUND

The Second Temple Era spanned 420 years, ending with the Roman destruction of the Holy Temple in 70 c.e. For the most part, this was an era of great political upheaval and religious strife. There was the constant threat of invasion from nations near and far. For much of this period, Judea was under foreign domination. There was the continual struggle for supremacy between the religious and political leaders. For much of this period, there was also the constant internal religious rivalry between the rabbinical Pharisees and the revisionist Sadducees.

The one radiant period of peace and tranquility was during the ten-year reign of Queen Shlomis Alexandra (76-66 b.c.e.). Shlomis Alexandra succeeded her husband King Yannai. Together with her brother Rabbi Shimon ben Shetach, she brought political and religious harmony to the land. The queen raised a strong army to defend the land. Rabbi Shimon ben Shetach built up a public *yeshivah* system throughout the land; every child was given an education. During these years the land was blessed. No enemy dared invade. Religious and moral ideals flourished. The economy prospered.

But Queen Shlomis was growing old and infirm, and her reign was coming to an end. She had two sons. The older son, Hyrkanus, was meek by nature and would be an ineffective successor to the throne. The greedy ambition of the younger son, Aristobulus, made him an unsuitable candidate as well. The Sages, sensing the likelihood of civil unrest, withdrew from the torrid political debate.

Upon the queen's death, the populace was divided as to who should be the successor to the throne. Bloody riots ensued, and the country was plunged into civil war. In order to spare their innocent countrymen further upheaval, the two brothers agreed to involve the great Roman general Pompey as a mediator. He would decide who was to be king. Pompey chose the docile Hyrkanus, intending to make him a puppet and Judea another province of the expanding Roman Empire.

Many Jews, faithful to Aristobulus, refused to accept Pompey's decision. Fighting broke out in Jerusalem. The Temple became a fortress for the rebellious faction. In 63 b.c.e., Pompey's troops entered the Holy City and put down the rebellion. Hyrkanus was installed as the puppet king and High Priest. Aristobulus was taken prisoner. The revolutionaries were executed. By allowing Pompey to become involved in the internal affairs of the Holy Land, Hyrkanus and Aristobulus had inadvertently given Judea into the hands of the Roman Empire.

Judea was heavily taxed by Rome and placed under the general jurisdiction of the Roman proconsul of Syria and Judea. A Roman governor of Judea was appointed. Though there were several attempts by the Jews to revolt against the abuses of the Roman proconsuls and governors, for the most part, the Jews endured the hardships with some degree of dignity.

In order to quell the spirit of Jewish nationalism, Judea was divided into five states, the *Sanhedrin* was officially disbanded and forced to convene in secret, and foreigners were brought into the land in an attempt to build up a non-Jewish majority.

By 66 c.e., the Jews in many of the coastal cities were treated as unwanted outsiders. They suffered the taunts of the Europeans who had migrated there. The despised Jews became the victims of murder and robbery. The Roman governor of Judea, Florius, imprisoned any Jew who brought a claim against a foreigner, whether or not the claim was justified. To further infuriate the Jews, Florius raided the Temple treasury for his own personal gain. He encouraged Roman soldiers to instigate riots in the Jewish quarters. On one day in 66 c.e., 3,600 Jews were killed in the city of Jerusalem.

Florius was hoping that the Jews of Jerusalem would attempt to avenge the slaughter. That way he could justify the mass killing of the entire Jewish population, loot their possessions and seize the Holy Temple. To his dismay, the Jews organized a march seeking to make peace with the governor. The Roman soldiers, lusting for blood, charged into the crowd of marchers, killing many Jews. The soldiers continued the forward assault battling their way to the Temple Mount.

Many Jews had gathered in the Temple to block the entrances, and the Roman soldiers retreated. The governor Florius, fearing possible retribution from the proconsul, went back to his estate in Caesarea. Florius had pushed the images of the murderers and riots to the back of his mind, but the Jews would not and could not forget. The first Revolt against Rome had begun.

Riots against the Romans erupted throughout the land. The proconsul Cestius Gallus was uncertain if the riots were only against the governor Florius or if they were aimed against Rome. In either event, the turmoil threatened Roman dominion. Cestius Gallus brought many troops with him to subdue Jerusalem. On the eighth day of *Cheshvan*, 66 c.e., Cestius Gallus suffered a humiliating and total defeat.

In Rome, word of the humiliation was met with raging hostility. Emperor Nero sent his most able general, Vespasian, with 60,000 Roman soldiers to quell the revolt in Judea. The initial military campaigns of Vespasian were centered in the northern Galilee. The untrained Jewish revolutionaries were no match for the disciplined Roman soldiers. One by one, the cities of the Galilee fell into Roman hands.

Vespasian now set his eye upon the Holy City, Jerusalem.

CHAPTER I
THE ENEMY WITHIN

KAMTZA AND BAR KAMTZA
66 C.E.

This is the tragic story of the downfall of a nation. It is the story of a once proud and noble people reduced to a nation of wanderers, beggars and slaves, of a people, once admired and revered, who became the object of scorn and hatred. It is the story of the Jewish nation. How did the Lord's chosen people become the Lord's rejected children? The Sages relate a story. It is a story of only a single incident, but it reveals the moral infection that invaded the Jewish spirit, culminating with the people's fall from grace.

A certain Jew had a friend named Kamtza and an enemy named Bar Kamtza. The Jew made a large feast and instructed his servant to invite Kamtza. The servant mistakenly invited Bar Kamtza. Bar Kamtza put on his finest clothes and attended the feast, assuming the Jew had forgiven their past rivalries.

When the Jew who hosted the feast found Bar Kamtza present, he demanded that Bar Kamtza leave at once.

"What are you doing here?" he fumed. "You tell tales and false stories about me, and you have the audacity to partake of my food and drink?"

"Since I am here," Bar Kamtza replied, "allow me to stay. I will pay for whatever I eat and drink."

The Jew angrily refused the offer.

"Then allow me to pay half the cost of the entire feast," pleaded Bar Kamtza.

"No," answered the stubborn Jew.

"Then I am willing to pay the full cost of the whole feast, but do not embarrass me any more," begged Bar Kamtza.

The unyielding Jew had Bar Kamtza dragged from the feast and thrown into the streets.

Bar Kamtza stood up, brushed the dust from his clothing and shouted with indignation, "O great and worthy Rabbi Zechariah ben Avkulas, you were present at this feast and yet you did not come to my defense. You, too, are party to my degradation and embarrassment. You remained silent. You, too, will regret what happens."

Bar Kamtza went to Emperor Nero and told him that the Jews were planning a rebellion against Rome.

"How do I know that to be true?" Nero asked.

"Send an offering to the Temple and see if it will be accepted as it has been in days past," Bar Kamtza said.

Nero sent a fine specimen of a calf for a burnt offering with Bar Kamtza, along with a delegation of Romans to accompany him. During the journey, Bar Kamtza secretly made a blemish on the animal, in effect disqualifying the animal as a sacrifice. When Bar Kamtza and the Roman delegation appeared with the offering at the Temple gates, the rabbis were inclined to accept the defective animal, so as not to offend the emperor. However, Rabbi Zechariah ben Avkulas insisted that a blemished animal could not be offered. The rabbis, realizing that Bar Kamtza had made the blemish on the animal to disqualify it, sought to kill Bar Kamtza.

"Is the punishment for inflicting a blemish the death penalty?" said Rabbi Zechariah. "Surely not. Let Bar Kamtza go back and tell Rome what happened. We have nothing to fear."

The delegation returned to Rome and told the emperor that his offering had not been accepted. Emperor Nero was furious, and the ramifications of his fury brought about one of the darkest chapters in our long and torturous history. But who was responsible for the consequence? Was it the carelessness of the servant who had invited the wrong person? Was it Bar Kamtza, who had spread false stories about a fellow Jew and told the emperor false tales against his people? Was it the stubbornness of the Jew who had given the party? Or perhaps, was it the condoning silence of Rabbi Zechariah ben Avkulas, the rabbi who had attended the feast? Truly a moral and philosophical riddle. Let us hear the rest of the tragic tale as it unfolds, and then we shall know who the guilty party really was.

Rioting filled the towns of Judea. The abuses and torments of the Roman governors were more than the Jews could bear. Private property was deemed the personal estate of the governor. Even the Temple treasury was raided. The populace was impelled to riot to reject these excesses. The Roman emperor, Nero, would not tolerate the rebelliousness of the Jews, no matter who was to blame. When Nero heard that the priests had refused to accept his Temple offering, he was convinced that Judea was not merely rioting against the excesses of the Roman governor, but was in fact rebelling against the Roman Empire.

The emperor sent Roman troops under the capable leadership of Vespasian Flavius to quell the rebellion. Vespasian's troops conquered the north of Israel. He then set his army against the Holy City. The people, sensing impending doom, began searching for the cause of their great misfortune. Most felt the blame rested with the servant whose carelessness in inviting Bar Kamtza to the feast triggered the sequence of unfortunate events. This explanation attributed the horrors that were to follow to some hapless mistake. Immoral infractions and social decadence played no part in the populace's responsibility of their misfortunes. Divine Providence and retribution played no part.

Some of the more learned blamed Bar Kamtza for attending the party. The custom in the Holy City was that one did not attend a feast unless extended an invitation

above: *Emperor Nero and his mother Agrippina*
right: *Vespasian*

twice, lest a mistake had been made. Bar Kamtza had attended the festivities after receiving only one invitation. The customs and proprieties of the Jewish people were to be guarded and treasured. Bar Kamtza did not guard this treasure carefully.

Other scholars blamed the tolerance of Rabbi Zechariah ben Avkulas. He had attended the party. He had witnessed Bar Kamtza's degradation and did not speak out. A rabbi must speak out against any injustice or misdeed. To remain silent is to condone. By Divine Providence, it fell to Rabbi Zechariah to deny acceptance of the emperor's blemished sacrifice. It would be his denial that would be reported to the emperor Nero.

Many Jews of the Holy Land were filled with the zealous spirit of rebellion. They sought to throw off the oppressive yoke of Roman dominion. Whether the Lord's blessing was given or not did not matter, only rebellion mattered. The rabbis remained silent, and to be silent is to condone. Silence wrought the destruction of the Lord's House and the devastation of our homeland.

THE ZEALOTS
68 C.E.

The Galilee had fallen; the north was in Roman hands. The Jewish general, Yochanan ben Levi of Gush Chalav, fled southward to Jerusalem. Yochanan, an ignoble person by birth and a bandit by trade, was a most unscrupulous man, with falsehoods and deceit as his second nature. This bloodthirsty savage arrived in the Holy City, claiming he had merely withdrawn his troops from the north.

"To risk Jewish lives for the defense of Gush Chalav would be irresponsible, so I came with my troops to the Holy City to regroup," he told the unsuspecting inhabitants, hiding the truth of the impending doom that threatened our nation. "Not even if the Romans grew wings could they scale the walls of Jerusalem. We have worn them down severely in the Galilee, and their engines of war are useless. We must fight them, for victory will be ours!"

Many of the youth were drawn to his boastful and provocative talk. The sober older men saw through the lies and bragging, and they began to mourn for the city as though it had already fallen.

Confusion and turmoil prevailed in Jerusalem. Should they fight the Roman invaders or surrender? The nation was torn apart. In Jewish homes, this gnawing question disrupted family harmony. Closest friends and dearest relatives severed ties. Factionalism reigned. The militant and revolutionary young silenced the old and cautious. Brash young men verbally and physically attacked those more prudent. Anarchy ruled the city.

"Oh, to be captured by the pagan Romans rather than by our fellow countrymen," the elders bemoaned.

The warmongering bandits called themselves Zealots. They traveled in small bands, pillaging the countryside. They wrought more havoc upon their fellow Jews than upon the Roman enemy.

As the countryside to the east, north and west fell into Roman hands, the Jewish refugees sought asylum in Jerusalem. The Holy City became an overcrowded haven, and the Zealots were like a plague in their midst. Men of stature, men of eminence, men of reason were all opposed to the Zealots. One by one, these great men were captured, imprisoned, tortured and killed. Terror filled the streets. The people were no longer concerned about the threat of the Romans; rather, the threat of the Zealots occupied their thoughts. And so, they feared for their safety in the safe haven of Jerusalem.

Jerusalem was held in a siege of terror. The Zealots rose quickly to power, even appointing their own High Priest, thus gaining access to the Holy Temple. The Zealots chose an ignorant man, Phanni ben Shmuel, as High Priest. They placed the priestly garments upon him and taught him how to behave. He was like an untrained actor standing before a discerning audience. The Zealots looked on with mockery and jest. The other priests looked away, bemoaning the degradation of the Temple service, tears flowing from their eyes.

During this trying time, Rabban Shimon ben Gamliel the Elder convened a mass assembly to arouse the people to reject the Zealots and find ways to regain authority over the city and the Temple. One of the participants, Chanan, the legitimate High Priest, a man of noble ancestry and bearing, stood up in front of the assemblage.

With tears in his eyes and facing the Holy Sanctuary, he said, "It would have been better to have died than to witness the Temple defiled by Jewish murderers. Why do I cling to life so dearly? Would it not be nobler to face death, which would shed glory, rather than to stand in silence and shame? When we witness injustice, why are we silent? When we see murder, why are we silent? When we watch the Temple being defiled, why are we silent? When we find tyranny, why then are we surprised? We have allowed it to happen. The blame lies not with the tyrants but with ourselves. Shall we wait for the Romans to deliver us from this tragedy? Some of you favor war against the Romans. But would they be more tyrannical than these dreaded Zealots? The Zealots are aptly named, for they pursue evil and corruption with zeal. If need be, I will go alone and fight these seditious men, if not for my sake, then for the sake of the Lord and His Sanctuary."

With these words, Chanan the High Priest aroused the people to fight against the Zealots. What they lacked in military skill they made up in sheer determination. The Holy City became a battleground for civil war. The Temple became the fortress of the Zealots. Chanan thought it sacrilegious to attack the Temple, so he surrounded it with six thousand armed men, dedicated and pure. They formed a human barrier and besieged the Temple.

The desperate Yochanan of Gush Chalav sent word to the Edomites in southern Judea to come and save the Holy City from this civil strife. The Edomites, though they had converted to Judaism centuries earlier, were an unruly people with an appetite for battle and revolution. They despised the noblemen, the wealthy and, even more so, the Romans. Yochanan told the Edomites that Chanan was preparing to turn over the Holy City to the Romans. They must come and deliver the city from its impending fate.

The Edomites entered Jerusalem and confronted the six thousand men who had surrounded the Zealot stronghold, the Temple. The six thousand bravely faced the Edomites before them and the Zealots behind. But the slaughter was great, and the blood of the six thousand flowed across the outer Temple Courtyard. The Edomites, in a frenzy for more blood, ran through the city streets, butchering and plundering. Young aristocrats were tortured to force them to join the fight against Rome. Twelve thousand young men perished rather than join the Zealots and their Edomite brigands.

During these riots, Chanan the High Priest was murdered. Some say that the destruction of the Jewish country began on the day that Chanan was killed, for he was the hope of the noble and wise.

The Zealots assembled the Grand *Sanhedrin* in the Temple Courts. Yochanan ordered the trial of Zechariah ben Baruch, one of the leaders of the anti-Zealot uprising.

Yochanan accused Zechariah of plotting to surrender the Holy City into the hands of Rome. Zechariah addressed the court.

"My only crime was to love my nation, my city and my Lord," he said. "How dare these Zealot barbarians defile what we hold so precious and dear? How dare they commit murder and mayhem while we sit idly by? If my cry is punishable by this court, then let it be so."

The men of the Grand *Sanhedrin* were sympathizers of Zechariah and the murdered Chanan, so they voted for his acquittal. The Zealots were outraged, and they rose up and slaughtered Zechariah in the Temple Court, flinging his body into the Kidron Valley below. The Zealots then turned against the members of the *Sanhedrin* and, hitting them with their swords, drove them out of the Temple Courtyard in disgrace.

PANGS OF HUNGER
69 C.E.

Not far from Jerusalem stood a formidable fortress called Masada. Built a hundred years earlier by King Herod of Judea as a royal refuge, it was now in the hands of the radical Jewish revolutionaries called the Sicarikon or "dagger carriers." They raided the neighboring town of Ein Gedi and murdered seven hundred of its Jewish inhabitants in order to gain more supplies for their fortress. This happened during the feast of Passover, the day we celebrate freedom from tyranny.

At this time, Shimon ben Giora, a leader of a troop of bandits that roamed the Judean desert, joined the radical Sicarikon at Masada. Shimon wished to dispose of the Zealot leader Yochanan in Jerusalem, for he had ambitions to be the leader of the revolution against Rome. Shimon marched toward Jerusalem, capturing every village and town in his path, including Hebron, the most ancient of cities, where our Patriarchs are buried.

Some of Yochanan's Zealots managed to kidnap the wife of Shimon. Gleefully, they brought her back to Jerusalem as though they had captured Shimon himself. Now, they thought, the distraught Shimon would surrender and yield to Yochanan's forces. But to the contrary, Shimon was enraged. With vengeful determination, he marched towards Jerusalem and camped outside the walls. People from the city, unaware of Shimon's intentions, went out to gather herbs and firewood. Many were captured. Some were murdered. Others had their hands cut off and were sent into the city where they were ordered to say that Shimon swore that a similar punishment would be inflicted upon every inhabitant of Jerusalem unless Shimon's wife was restored to him. The Zealots were terrified and returned Shimon's wife.

Shimon was not satisfied with the mere return of his wife; he wanted the entire city. Shimon and his brigands invaded Jerusalem and ransacked the homes of the wealthy, sowing murder and mayhem. In a state of demented stupor, Shimon's men dressed in bizarre clothing, braided their hair and doused themselves with perfume, and polluted the sacred streets with their insane behavior.

Shimon's Sicarikon captured the Holy City, forcing Yochanan's Zealots to withdraw into the Temple. The Temple, because of its elevated position, proved to be an ideal fortress. Yochanan erected four towers in the Temple to ensure his superior position. One tower was constructed in the northeastern corner of the Temple. A second was built in the middle of the western wall overlooking the street below. A third tower, in the southwestern corner, stood above the Lower City, and the fourth tower, in the south, was built next to the Place of the Trumpeting, where the Temple priests customarily sounded the *shofar* to signal the onset of *Shabbos*, the day of peace and tranquility, a day set aside to commemorate the supreme reign of the Lord and harmony among men. In this place, the rebellious Yochanan positioned his soldiers with crossbows and catapults aimed at their fellow Jews.

One of the Zealots, Eleazar ben Shimon, considered himself superior to Yochanan. He convinced a number of his fellow Zealots to join him and withdraw from the outer Temple Courtyard, held secure by Yochanan, into the inner Temple precincts. This area was higher than the outer courtyard and would offer a better strategic position. The Temple storehouses would supply food and drink, and the holy vessels could be fashioned into instruments of war.

Shimon commanded the city, Yochanan had the outer Temple Courtyard, and Eleazar now controlled the inner Temple precinct. The citizenry was in a state of confusion and despair. Jerusalem had become like a raving beast driven by starvation to consume its own flesh.

Yochanan held the most vulnerable position. His men

were locked in place in the outer Temple Courtyard. They could not move outside because of Shimon's troops below, they could not move inside the Sanctuary because of Eleazar's troops above, and so the attacks centered on Yochanan's troops in the outer Temple Courtyard. The more determined citizens still sought access to the Holy Temple in order to bring their sacrifices and to perform the Temple service. Even more miraculous, they were given permission to enter after undergoing a thorough search to make certain they bore no arms. After gaining access to the Temple Courtyard, the rivalry and fighting continued around them. Many innocents were felled by arrows and missiles. Priests and petitioners lay on the ground near the Altar, their own blood mingling with the blood of the sacrifices. The Holy Sanctuary had become a cemetery. The area of the city surrounding the Temple was reduced to ashes, each faction having incinerated the storehouses and supplies of the other.

During the campaign of Vespasian against Jerusalem, the Sages intoned the words of the forsaken Job, "Remove the turban, lift off the crown." For years, the custom had been for a bridegroom to wear a splendid crown at his wedding feast. A groom of the aristocracy would don a crown fashioned from the finest crystal. The common citizen would wear upon his head a ring of myrtle branches adorned with roses. But there was no longer cause for such excessive rejoicing and merriment. The Sages foresaw that the High Priest would soon no longer wear his priestly turban; the divine decree had been sealed. Why, then, should the bridegroom wear his crown? The Grand *Sanhedrin* forbade the crown of the groom. The rhythmic sound of the tambourine, a musical instrument favored by the Romans, was also forbidden, and it was no longer heard at Jewish celebrations.

Wondering if the campaign in Judea would meet with success, Nero sought some omen. He shot an arrow into the air toward the east, and when it landed, it pointed toward Jerusalem. He shot another arrow, this time toward the west, and when it landed, it too pointed to Jerusalem. In all, four arrows were shot in the four directions, and each landed pointing to the Holy City. While Nero pondered the significance of this strange occurrence, he saw a Jewish lad passing by.

"What did you learn in school today?" the emperor demanded of the lad.

Reluctantly, the young student answered, "We learned the verse of the prophet Ezekiel, 'And I shall seek revenge against the descendants of Esau.'"

Nero said, "The Holy Blessed One seeks to destroy the Nation of Israel and His Holy House, and to place the blame with Rome, the descendant of Esau. I shall have no part of this."

Nero gave up his royal position and joined the ranks of the Jews as a convert. With the sudden disappearance of the emperor, Rome was in a turmoil. Civil war broke out. Different factions sought to claim the royal vacancy. The same disease that inflicted Judea had spread to her enemy.

At this time, three noble and wealthy men resided in the Holy City. They were Nakdimon ben Gorion, Ben Kalba Savua and Ben Tzitzis Hakeses. Nakdimon was considered worthy that the sun would shine on his account. Ben Kalba Savuah was generous to the needy, who were constant guests in his home. Ben Tzitzis had long fringes that trailed upon cushions that were placed upon the ground. He was admired and respected by the nobility of Rome. One of these three was able to supply the Holy City with all the grain that was needed. The second had wine, oil and salt. The third had firewood. Between them, Jerusalem could have withstood a siege of twenty-one years, but it was the storehouse containing these wares that the Zealot revolutionaries burned. They destroyed the only hope of survival. Starvation began to rip apart the very fiber of the Holy City.

Residing in Jerusalem was Marsa, the daughter of Baisus. Marsa was a member of one of the wealthiest families in the Holy City, but her wealth was of no use during the famine. She sent her manservant out to purchase some fine flour. The servant wandered through the markets of the devastated city for hours, returning to his mistress empty-handed.

"There is no fine flour to be had, only white flour," he said.

"Then fetch me some of that," Marsa said.

Again the servant wandered the streets searching for white flour, but he returned to his mistress empty-handed. "There is no white flour to be had, only coarse flour."

"Then get me some coarse flour," Marsa said.

Late in the afternoon, he returned to his mistress and said, "There is no longer any coarse flour, but barley can still be had."

Marsa sent her servant out again, and once more, he returned empty-handed. Marsa was so distraught that she herself set out to find something to eat.

Being of aristocratic birth, Marsa's soles had never touched a bare floor, but now, because her feet had become swollen and sore from hunger, she was unable to bear the weight of her sandals. Barefoot, she walked through the streets of Jerusalem. Each step was a painful process, painful because of the sores and painful because of the degradation she suffered. Jerusalem, too, suffered degradation. Its once beautiful streets had become littered with filth and decay. Marsa's foot touched some of the dung that defiled the filthy streets. The shock caused her to become faint, and she fell upon the ground. Her hand lay across a rotting fig with the juice sucked from it.

The holy sage Rabbi Tzaddok fasted forty years to forestall the fate of the Holy City. Rabbi Tzaddok's body was so wasted that anything he swallowed could be seen as it passed down his throat. When he wished to restore himself, he would suck the juice from a fig. It was one of these figs that Marsa's hand was now touching. She placed the half-eaten, decaying fig in her mouth. Her delicate body began to tremble in revulsion. She took her jewels and gold and cast them into the street, saying, "Of what value are these now?" She fell back and died.

In the end, when Jerusalem fell, it was not because the Roman siege had led to mass starvation. Had there not been this factional rivalry, had the Jews not destroyed the great supplies of grain, fruit and drink, Jerusalem could have held out. The city would have survived. The people would not have been slaughtered and exiled. The Temple would not have been destroyed. It may be said that it was the

Jewish people who had brought about their own miserable fate.

The old men and women of the city walked about in a dazed state. Human and animal carcasses littered the streets. The people prayed for the Romans to deliver them from their misery. There was no place to bury the dead, for there was no cemetery within the city. If anyone tried to leave the city to bury a dear one or a fallen comrade, it was assumed that he was plotting to surrender to the Roman enemy, and he was duly executed. The shouts of the combatants rang through the streets during the day. The moans of the mourners, borne by the wind, filled the streets at night. Jerusalem became a city of horrifying sounds—sounds of anguish, sounds of despair.

The sage Rabbi Yochanan ben Zakai was passing through the streets of the Holy City. He noticed some men huddled around a pot set over a small fire. They were boiling straw. When the straw was boiled, they passed the pot around and took turns gratefully sipping the water.

"How fallen is the nation of Israel!" Rabbi Yochanan exclaimed. "They share the same food as the animals of the market and eat with pleasure. How much longer must our people suffer?"

One of the generals of the Zealots was Abba Sikarah, the nephew of Rabbi Yochanan ben Zakai. The rabbi sent word that his nephew should meet him in a secluded place. "How long will you cause the people to die of starvation? Would not a surrender to Rome save our people, the Holy City and the Lord's Temple?"

"Noble uncle, what you say may be true," Abba Sikarah

replied. "But if my comrades hear these words, both of us will surely be slain."

Rabbi Yochanan ben Zakai pleaded with his nephew to devise some plan for the rabbi to meet with the Roman general Vespasian. Perhaps some good could be accomplished.

Abba Sikarah thought a moment, then he said, "Uncle, pretend that you are ill. Place some spoiled meat on your bed next to you and tell your students to spread the word that you have died. Let your students carry the bier outside the city walls for a proper burial. Let no one else carry it, for they will know that you are still alive."

Rabbi Yochanan did as his nephew instructed. His students, Rabbi Eliezer and Rabbi Yehoshua, carried the bier. As they approached the city gates to go outside, one of the Zealot guards approached them.

"Let us pierce the body with a lance to make certain he is dead," the guard said.

Abba Sikarah, who was nearby, said, "The Romans will mock us, saying that we murder our sages. Besides, can you not smell the odor of death that comes from this bier?"

And so, the gates of the city were opened for the funeral procession, and the bier was carried to a burial vault outside the city. The students left the holy teacher alone and went back into the city. Later that evening, Rabbi Yochanan ben Zakai left the vault and made his way to the camp of Vespasian.

"Peace unto you, Caesar, peace unto you," Rabbi Yochanan greeted the general.

"Rabbi, you deserve to be killed on two accounts,"

Vespasian angrily responded. "One, I am not the Caesar, and yet you mockingly address me as such. Second, if you really think me to be the Caesar, why did you not come sooner?"

"Mighty Vespasian, you are the Caesar, for if you were not a king, Jerusalem would not fall into your hands," Rabbi Yochanan answered. "You asked why did I not come sooner? Because of the Zealots in our midst. They do not allow us to leave the city gates."

"Are not the Zealots like a serpent coiled around a jar of sweet honey?" Vespasian asked. "You should have broken the jar to remove the serpent. You should have torn down the walls of the city. They would have no place to hide, and together we could have removed this serpent from your midst."

Rabbi Yochanan did not respond.

Meanwhile, a messenger from Rome came into the camp and called out, "Let all those who are present arise. The nobles of Rome have proclaimed our mighty and noble general, the illustrious Vespasian Flavius, as emperor. Long live Vespasian. Long live the emperor."

The newly-appointed emperor was impressed with the foresight of the sage and granted him three requests. Rabbi Yochanan ben Zakai realized that Vespasian was in a euphoric mood, but the joy would soon pass. The realities of the revolt would be on his mind, and any grand request would be forgotten or ignored. Therefore, the sage asked the emperor for three things that were likely to be granted. He asked that the rabbis in the college in Yavneh be spared, that the family of Rabban Gamliel be spared and that physicians be brought to heal Rabbi Tzaddok, whose health had deteriorated because of his fasting. The three requests were granted.

Vespasian departed from the battlefront to assume his position in Rome. He left his son, Titus Flavius, to assume the military command of the Roman troops in Judea.

While Jerusalem was tearing itself apart, Titus Flavius, the commander-in-chief of all the Roman forces in Judea, the son of the emperor Vespasian, marched toward the Holy City. He led the fifth, tenth, twelfth and fifteenth legions, sixty thousand battle-hardened legionnaires, to Givat Shaul, about three and one half miles north of Jerusalem. In the vanguard were the generals and their attendants. Behind them were the road builders and surveyors. Next were the carriers of the supplies, and then the troops. Then came Titus, the commander-in-chief, escorted by his lancers and selected soldiers, followed by the cavalry. Then came the machines and engines of war with the standard bearers and trumpet blowers. Last were the servants, the Arab mercenaries and the rear guards. Any man of reasonable faculties, upon seeing such impressive might, would feel compelled to surrender out of sheer terror. But the

Titus Flavius

quarrelling inhabitants of Jerusalem, unheedful of the Sages, were not men of reasonable faculties.

Titus chose six hundred select horsemen to accompany him to reconnoiter the strength of the city and to test the determination of the Jews. Titus and the six hundred rode from the north to Jerusalem. Their advance went unchallenged. As they neared the northern wall of the city opposite the Tomb of Helena, a band of Jewish revolutionaries ran out of the Women's Gate and split the cavalry in two. The larger group retreated and Titus remained with but a few horsemen. The Jews were in front of him, the gardens to his rear. The Roman commander was trapped. Titus reared his horse and charged into the contingent of

The Tomb of Queen Heleni, north of ancient Jerusalem. The first skirmish between Titus and the Zealots in the Holy City took place in front of this tomb.

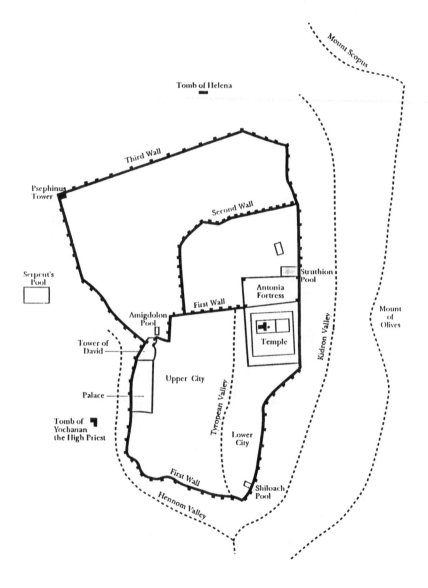

Map 1

Jews. The Jews fired arrows and hurled spears at the Roman general. As if by divine decree, not a single arrow or spear touched him. Indeed, Titus managed to trample some of his enemies and join the larger group of horsemen who had retreated. (Map 1)

Had the Jews been noble and wise, as history has always portrayed them, they would have realized that it was not in their power to subdue the Romans. But these Jews were intoxicated with their small victory, which gave them false hope and confidence.

During that evening, the Roman legions joined Titus. Together they marched to Mount Scopus, about half a mile northeast of the city. From its summit, the grandeur and radiance of the Temple could be seen. Titus set up his camp on Scopus with the twelfth legion. He stationed the fifth legion a thousand feet to the rear. The tenth and fifteenth legions were quartered on top of the Mount of Olives, less than half a mile east of the city. The Holy Temple was situated directly across and to the west of the Mount of Olives. The Kidron Valley, a deep ravine, separated the Temple and the Mount of Olives. Recognizing the Roman threat, the warring factions within the city made an unholy alliance. "Are we brave only against ourselves?" they asked.

They planned a joint attack against the legions on the Mount of Olives. The Romans were preoccupied with establishing their camp, never imagining that the Jews would cross the Kidron Valley to attack. The Romans had set aside their weapons and were not prepared for battle. The first wave of Jews to invade the camp caught the Romans unaware. The Romans quickly dispersed and fled.

The Mount of Olives. At the foot of the mountain is the Kidron Valley. Ancient tombs line the valley. The tomb with the round spire is Absalom's Monument. Immediately to the left and in back of Absalom's tomb is the burial site of the Judean king Yehoshafat. The tomb to the right with the pyramid on top is the burial site of the First Temple prophet and priest Zechariah. To the left of Zechariah's tomb is the burial vault of the priestly clan of Chezir.

Other Jews, watching from the eastern city wall, were encouraged to join the battle. Titus, hearing the commotion from nearby Scopus, rallied his troops to chase the Jewish revolutionaries down into the valley.

The Romans had the high position on the slopes of Scopus and the Mount of Olives. The Jews were in the valley below, and many were killed. Fleeing up the slope toward the eastern city wall, the Jews came to an elevation equal with that of the Romans, with the Kidron Valley between them. The Jews turned, shooting back many arrows at the

Romans. Panic gripped the Romans, who did not expect the fleeing Jews to turn around and fight. However, the Romans quickly regained their military composure and returned the volley of arrows with their own. Titus rode among his legions shouting words of encouragement to buoy the spirits of his men. Night soon fell. The Romans withdrew to the top of the mountains, and the Jews withdrew into the city.

CHAPTER TWO
THE BATTLE FOR JERUSALEM

TITUS
NISSAN, 70 C.E.

The Romans maintained their positions atop Scopus to the northeast and atop the Mount of Olives to the east. The Zealots remained uncharacteristically quiet within the city. The festival of Passover was approaching. Yochanan, who controlled the outer Temple courts, and Eleazar, who controlled the inner precincts, declared an amnesty for the upcoming holiday. Anyone seeking entrance to the Temple to offer the traditional Paschal sacrifice would be admitted without any scrutiny.

The unscrupulous Yochanan took advantage of this truce and disguised his men as ordinary citizens. They carried their weapons beneath their robes. That Passover Eve, the Temple courts were crowded. Yochanan's Zealots ripped off their outer robes, took out their weapons, and shouting like wounded beasts, they ran through the Temple. Unable to distinguish between Eleazar's faithful and the innocent citizens, the Zealots slaughtered both with equal abandon. Eleazar and many of his followers retreated to the tunnels below the Temple floor. Thus Yochanan regained control of the entire Temple Mount. When the refuge of Eleazar and his men was discovered, they were admitted into the upper Temple area and amnesty was granted.

Our ancestors celebrated the first Passover in Egypt. They remained in the safety of their homes while the Angel of Death wrought destruction upon the Egyptians on the outside. The last Passover to be commemorated by our people in the Holy Temple was that bloody day when Yochanan regained dominance over the sacred quarters. Yochanan, the Angel of Death, wrought his destruction upon our people in that most sacred of places. The Jewish nation was born under the sign of the sacrificial Paschal blood, and now the Paschal sacrifice was ended under the sign of Jewish blood.

Jerusalem was reduced to two revolutionary factions, Yochanan and his Zealots, with their headquarters on the Temple Mount, and Shimon and the Sicarikon in the city.

Titus now decided to move his camp closer to the city walls. The gardens and orchards outside the city to the north and west were uprooted. Every hill was leveled and every depression was filled so as not to hinder the movement of the horses and the machines of war. The leveling was from Scopus to the monuments of Herod near the Serpent's Pool. At this time, some of the Zealots were chased out from the northern Women's Gate. From atop the wall, some citizens pelted them with small stones. The Zealots were in a quandary. They could not run back into the city because of the barrage of stones, and they dared not run forward because the Romans were a few yards in front of them.

The citizens atop the wall called to the Romans, "Peace! Peace!"

The suspicious Titus ordered his troops not to approach the city for fear of some trick. Several of his troops, however, were unable to resist the easy capture of these revolutionaries. As they came close to the gate, the men on top of the wall put aside their stones and began hurling spears and large rocks at the Roman soldiers. In the meantime, the Zealots, who had pretended to have been ejected from the city, ran back inside the Women's Gate. Other Zealots ran out to attack the stunned Romans. Only after suffering heavy losses did the Romans manage to retreat to the Tomb of Helena.

Titus was angered at the insubordination of his soldiers. They had caused Rome to become a mockery. Their punishment was to be death. However, due to the urging of Titus' more faithful followers, their lives were spared. They pledged to follow every word their commander ordered and to display greater caution and courage.

It took four days for Titus to level the ground opposite the north and west wall. He pitched his own camp twelve hundred feet north of the Psephinus Tower. This one-hundred-ten-foot high structure was the tallest tower in the Holy City. Octagonally shaped, it was built onto the north-west corner of the city wall. From its summit, one could see the hills of Jordan to the east and the glistening sea to the west. And from its summit, the Jews watched the Romans with great apprehension.

Another camp was pitched twelve hundred feet west of the western city wall, across from the Fortress of David. The tenth legion remained on the Mount of Olives (Map 2).

Titus sent some horsemen to inspect the city walls to determine his point of attack. After the inspection was made, Titus decided to base the attack opposite the Tomb of Yochanan the High Priest and to assault the city from the west of the Fortress of David. The ground was the most level at this point, and from here he planned to break through the wall, capture the Upper City and march to the Antonia Fortress. The Antonia was adjacent to the northern part of the Holy Temple. In order to capture the Temple Mount, the Antonia had to be in Roman control.

The Fortress of David

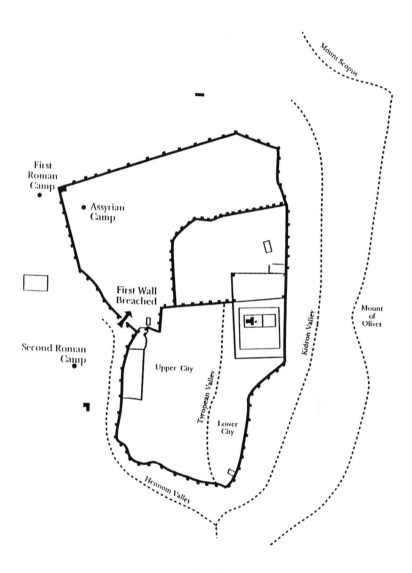

First Roman Camp

• Assyrian Camp

First Wall Breached

Second Roman Camp

Upper City

Tyropean Valley

Lower City

Hennom Valley

Kidron Valley

Mount Scopus

Mount of Olives

Map 2

FROM THE MIDRASH [53]

The remains of a walkway that led from the Upper City to the Western Wall.

Titus ordered that the suburbs be destroyed and the trees felled in order to build three ramps against the western city wall. The war machines and movable towers would be pushed up the ramps, and the walls would be battered in. Javelin hurlers, archers, soldiers with crossbows and the stone-throwing catapults were stationed near the builders to prevent the revolutionaries from attacking.

Undaunted, Shimon's men marched from the city to attack the Romans and engage them in close combat. The Roman front lines were protected by a line of soldiers holding wicker shields, and from the rear the Romans shot arrows, spears and stone missiles. Because of the Roman military superiority, the Jews had to retreat. The Romans catapulted large stone missiles over the walls. The stones whistled as they shot through the air.

The Jews perched atop the walls would look in the

direction of the sound, and as they saw the white projectiles coming at them they would yell, "Stone! Stone!"

The people would crouch down as the missiles shot harmlessly by. To frustrate the efforts of the Jews, the Romans darkened the stones so they could not be easily detected. The missiles began to inflict much injury to the Jews atop the walls. In spite of this, the Jews did not allow the Romans to build their ramps unmolested. With much daring and ingenuity, the revolutionaries tried to thwart

Roman Catapult

Javelin Shooter

Stone Hurler

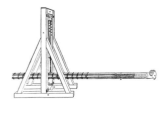

Battering Ram

the Romans' plans during the day and far into the night.

Even as the ramps were being built outside the city walls, Shimon and Yochanan continued their raids against each other. Shimon commanded fifteen thousand troops, including the Edomites, and sixty generals. Yochanan commanded eight thousand four hundred troops and twenty-two generals. Meanwhile, three battering rams were drawn up to the western city wall, and their mighty hammering began. The city shook as if hit by an earthquake. Once again urged by fear, Shimon and Yochanan declared a truce. Together, they threw torches and stones down upon the Roman battle machines. A party of revolutionaries ran among the troops, creating much confusion. The Romans temporarily withdrew from their machines, and the Jews set them afire. But Titus rallied his troops, who then charged the Jews and managed to douse the fires. Twelve Jews were killed and one was captured. Titus ordered him to be crucified before the walls of the city as an example to the rest to surrender in despair.

During that battle, an Edomite general, whose name was also Yochanan, was killed when an arrow struck him in the chest. This Yochanan was admired for his bravery and distinguished for his cunning plans. His death caused much grief and dismay among the revolutionaries.

The next night, the Romans became alarmed by a most unexpected occurrence. Titus had ordered seventy-five-foot high wooden towers to be constructed and encased in iron. He commanded that they be moved to the top of the ramps so that the soldiers perched on top of them could repel the revolutionaries stationed atop the wall. In the middle of the night, a tower that was improperly constructed suddenly collapsed. The Romans, hearing the great crash, awoke in panic, thinking the enemy was upon them. Everyone ran for weapons. When they could neither see nor find the enemy, the panic and terror increased. Every soldier asked the other for the password, fearing the Jews had disguised themselves as Roman soldiers. Eventually, the panic subsided, and they realized what had happened.

Moveable Seige Tower

The following morning, the Romans placed javelin hurlers, archers and stone throwers on top of the remaining two towers. Battering rams were placed between the towers. The Jews were unwilling to stand atop the wall and throw stones at the battering rams for fear of the Romans atop the towers. And so the rams hammered away at the walls unhampered.

FIRST WALL BREACHED
7 IYAR, 70 C.E.

On the seventh day of *Iyar*, the battering rams broke through the wall (Map 2). Jerusalem was protected by three mighty walls. Originally, the city of Jerusalem had one wall

The Western City Wall. Titus first broke into Jerusalem at this point.

around it. As it expanded outward, new walls were built. Now, the outer wall had been breached. The revolutionaries withdrew behind the second wall. Between the outer wall and the second wall were the northern suburbs of the city. Upon gaining possession of these suburbs, the Romans destroyed the whole district.

Centuries earlier, during the period of the First Temple and the reign of the Judean king Hezkiah, the Assyrian general Sancherev camped in these quarters to wage war against the Jewish capital. An angel of the Lord came and annihilated the Assyrian army. Titus set up his new camp in the very quarters where Sancherev had camped. Perhaps, Titus thought, fortune would be kinder to him.

Yochanan commanded his troops from the Antonia Fortress and launched attacks to the north. Shimon commanded his faithful from the Tower of David and aimed his attacks toward the Tomb of Yochanan the High Priest in the west. Titus moved the battering rams opposite the middle tower of the northern section of the second wall. As the ram battered, the tower rocked. Several Jews who were hiding in the tower made their presence known to the Romans. They held their hands up high as if to surrender. One of them spoke.

"My name is Castor. There are ten men here, including me. Five of us wish to surrender; the others are afraid. Give me time to convince them, and we shall all come over to you."

Titus ordered the battering to stop. Meanwhile, Castor sent word to Shimon to send troops to the tower. As time passed, the Roman archers grew impatient. One shot an arrow which grazed Castor's nose. Castor picked up the arrow and held it skyward for Titus to see.

"Is this the treatment you promised me?" he asked.

Titus ordered one of his men to approach the tower and offer his apologies. Castor, sensing that Shimon's troops were not coming to rescue him, cast down a rock on the approaching Roman soldier. Titus, realizing that he had been tricked, was angry with himself. Directing his anger to the wall, he ordered that the battering ram be worked twice as fast, and soon the tower crashed.

With the collapse of the tower, the second wall had been breached (Map 3). In this section of the city were the wool shops, the pot makers and the clothes markets. The narrow, twisting streets were like a maze to those unfamiliar with the district.

Titus and one thousand legionnaires broke through the breach in the wall. Titus ordered them not to kill any man or burn any building, but rather to grant safe passage to anyone not bearing arms who wished to leave the city. The citizenry wanted to leave, but the revolutionaries took Titus' humanitarian gestures as a sign of weakness.

These Zealots believed that Titus' peaceful overtures were due to his inability to occupy the city securely. The revolutionary Zealots forbade anyone to surrender under pain of death. They fought doggedly against the Roman troops.

The labyrinthine streets were like a trap to the Romans, but to the Jews, this was their home. The foreigners stumbled through the twisting alleys. The Zealots darted in and out of narrow passageways and hurled arrows from the rooftops, attacking the Romans from a few yards away and escaping through the sewers below. The Zealots managed to drive the Roman soldiers back out through the breach in the second wall. The district was once again in Jewish hands.

The Zealots now believed they were invincible. Rome would never dare to strike again, and so they celebrated.

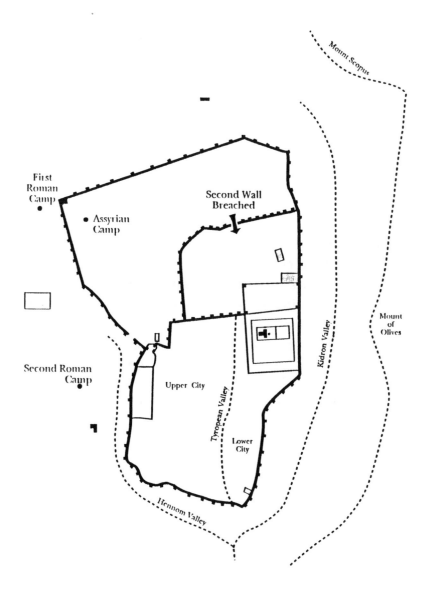

Map 3

But the festivities were dulled by the cries of the mourners in the city. The Romans had withdrawn, but the hunger was advancing. The Zealots had destroyed the grain and fruit supplies.

Northern City Invaded
17 Iyar, 70 c.e.

Since a breach had already been made in the second wall, the Romans found it relatively easy to enlarge the opening. By the seventeenth of *Iyar*, the entire northern section of the second wall had been torn down. Now Titus had undisputed control over the district. Garrisons were stationed to the south near the third, innermost wall of the city. Titus retired to his camp to plan his attack on the third and final wall protecting Jerusalem.

Titus decided to wait. The Jews were downcast at the loss of the second wall. Starvation was devastating the city. Time was on his side.

Emissaries arrived from Rome with the soldiers' pay. Titus made a grand spectacle of the payment to his troops. The soldiers polished their weapons and raised their banners. Their armor glistened in the morning sun. The Jews stood on top of the inner wall and gazed in awe. The troops paraded by to receive their gold and silver coins. After each soldier received his coin, he gleefully held it high. This grand display lasted for four days.

FAMINE AND DEFECTION
21 IYAR, 70 C.E.

Titus was growing restless. His troops were also anxious for battle. He divided them into two groups. The fifth and twelfth legions were to raise up two ramps thirty feet apart against the northern walls of the Antonia Fortress near the pool called Struthion. The tenth and fifteenth legions were to raise up two ramps against the western face of the inner wall near the pool called Amigdolon (Map 4). The task of Yochanan and his Zealots was to stave off the Antonia rampworks. The Jews occupying the higher position had by now become experts in using the stone catapults and crossbows they had captured. The Roman objective would not go unchallenged. Titus was concerned with his own reputation and the glory or shame he would bring to Rome.

The Amigdolon Pool. Built by the Judean king Chizkiyah, this cistern supplied the Fortress of David and the Temple with water. The Romans built assault ramps next to this pool.

Many Jewish citizens secretly planned

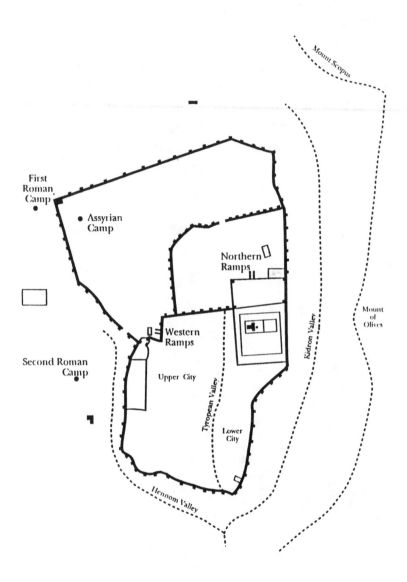

First
Roman
Camp

Assyrian
Camp

Northern
Ramps

Western
Ramps

Upper City

Second Roman
Camp

Tyropean Valley

Lower
City

Kidron Valley

Mount Scopus

Mount
of
Olives

Hennom Valley

Map 4

to surrender. They sold their possessions and treasures for a mere trifle. If the revolutionaries caught them carrying money or gems, they would know that a defection was planned. So these Jews swallowed their gold coins and gemstones. Those who made it to the Roman camps were granted safe passage to the countryside. Shimon and Yochanan kept a sharp lookout for these defectors. If the slightest doubt was cast upon anyone's motives, he was instantly put to death.

Inside the city, the famine increased day by day. Those who had private stores of food were accused of being deserters and murdered so that the revolutionaries could seize the supplies. Homes were ransacked, and the inhabitants were tortured to reveal where their grain was hidden. The physical conditions of the inhabitants were considered proof of whether or not food supplies were hidden. Many bartered all their possessions for a measure of grain—wheat if they were rich, barley if they were poor. They hid themselves in the basements to partake of the food. A few even dared to roast the grain. The odor of their prize would seep outside, and raiders would burst in and snatch the half-roasted food.

All human emotions yield to hunger, most of all, the sense of shame. Husbands ripped food away from their wives, and mothers snatched it out of the mouths of infants. As dear ones lay dying in their arms, they would not give them lifesaving nourishment.

If the brigands saw a locked door, they suspected that a meal was being served inside. The doors would be broken down, and they would burst in and grab the food from the jaws of those eating. Often the victims were choked to bring up the morsels they had swallowed. Had the revolutionary Zealots been driven by hunger, such actions might have been understandable. But they had their own supplies and stores. Because they wanted to increase their stores, they tortured the citizens to yield them their food. Any citizen who ate was considered a traitor to the revolutionary cause.

As the rampworks of Titus were nearing completion, a detachment of cavalry was sent to round up the Jews who had managed to slip out of the city to gather herbs and grasses for food. Those Jews, although in a position to defect, were afraid to do so for fear that their wives and children would be butchered by the Zealots, and when they were captured by the Romans, they tried to resist in order to get back into the city to their families; if not for the concern over their loved ones, they would have gladly defected.

The Romans assumed that their captives were revolutionaries, so they were flogged, tortured and, in the end, crucified before the walls of the city. Five hundred Jews were crucified every day. The Roman soldiers, out of rage and hatred, amused themselves by nailing their prisoners into all sorts of different positions and impaling many to a single cross. Their sport was hindered only by a lack of space for the crosses, because there were so many, and also by a lack of crosses, for the wood was needed for the rampworks.

The Zealots pulled the families of the crucified Jews to the tops of the city walls to show the fate of those seeking to defect. Some, because of the terrifying sight of the crosses bearing their loved ones, now willingly joined the Zealots. Others jumped over the walls, preferring to take their chances with crucifixion rather than face the horror of starvation.

Titus ordered that the hands of the defectors be severed and sent back into the city to convince Shimon to surrender. The Zealots mounted the walls and shouted their answer to the Romans.

"We prefer an honorable death to becoming mutilated Roman subjects. We are fighting for the Lord's sanctuary, and He is our ally. The Lord will defend us and make you a mockery." Such religious contentions and presumptions did the Zealots yell, along with insults.

At this time, Antiochus Epiphanes, son of the king of Commagene, came upon the scene. This most faithful servant to Rome led a large force of infantry called the Macedonian Brigade. Though they were not Macedonians, they were trained after the fashion of Alexander the Great of Macedonia. Antiochus was surprised to learn that Titus was reluctant to strike at the walls of the city.

"Can it be that this city half in ruins is an obstacle in the path of the mighty Titus?" he asked.

"The field is open to you," Titus replied with a smile. "Try your hand. Perhaps you are a more daring warrior than I."

Antiochus led his infantry against the walls of Jerusalem. The Zealots hailed a barrage of stones and arrows down upon them. Jews ran forth from the city gates and daringly attacked the so-called Macedonians. In defeat,

Antiochus led his men in retreat.

While his soldiers nursed their wounds, he looked toward the city and said, "It would take Alexander himself to conquer this city." Sobered by the experience, Antiochus led his troops away.

THE RAMPWORKS COLLAPSE
29 IYAR, 70 C.E.

The rampworks north of the Antonia Fortress were nearing completion. While these works were being constructed, Yochanan and his Zealots had dug a tunnel underneath the ramp. The great weight of the ramp rested directly on top of the roof of the tunnel, which was supported by great timbers. Yochanan smeared the wooden timbers with pitch and ignited them. As the supports were consumed by fire, the tunnel collapsed with a thundering crash and the rampworks fell in. A dense cloud of smoke issued forth, followed by leaping tongues of fire. It was as if a volcano had erupted.

At first, the Romans were startled and frightened, but when they realized what had happened, their spirits fell. What had seemed like an imminent victory was dashed by the cleverness of the Jews. The Romans drew back and silently watched the rising smoke, illuminated by the glow of the burning embers in the moonless nighttime sky.

The Zealots Attack
2 Sivan, 70 c.e.

Two days after Yochanan's attack on the northern rampworks, Shimon sent three of his bravest Zealots to burn the battering machines that were already being pulled up the western ramps. In the whole course of the war, the city produced none more heroic than these three, nor were there any others who inspired greater terror. Carrying torches, they sallied forth from the city gates as though they were running to greet friends. Attacked with volleys of arrows and missiles, they continued to run forward. They put the torches to the wooden battering rams. The fire caught. The three fought hand to hand with those Romans who tried to extinguish the fire. More Zealots ran out from the city and pursued the Romans to the very front lines of their camp.

Tunnel under the Temple Mount. Used as a refuge by the Jewish Zealots.

The sentries who guarded the front lines were forbidden by Roman law to leave their posts under penalty of death. Frightened by the running, shouting Jews, many sentries fled in confusion. A line of crossbows was quickly set up, and the Romans managed to stop the advancing Jews. Though the Romans possessed superior military skill and training, the Jews fought with daring and courage, not afraid to risk their lives. With great difficulty, the Romans prevented the total destruction of their camp.

CHAPTER III
THE SIEGE OF JERUSALEM

THE SIEGE BEGINS
3 SIVAN, 70 C.E.

Titus held a council of war with his officers. Some advised a full-scale assault against the city. Others were in favor of rebuilding the rampworks. Some thought that a siege wall should be constructed around the city so that hunger would take its course. Titus was not in favor of the mass assault, as the Jews were willing to die for their cause. Great numbers of Romans would be killed at the cost of victory. Nor did he favor reconstructing the rampworks, since materials were in low supply. The last option was chosen. A wall would be constructed around the entire city, blocking every exit. The city could not last long without food, for starvation had already taken a great toll.

Titus divided up the work. Each legion was given a section of wall to build. The troops were enthusiastic and undertook the task with glee. The various legions and companies made it a competitive sport to see who could complete their section of wall first.

In three days, the five mile long wall was built. Groups were set up to patrol the wall at night. The wall was like a hangman's noose around the neck of Jerusalem.

SCENES OF DEPRAVITY
6 SIVAN, 70 C.E

As the days passed, the victims of starvation increased. The rooftops were filled with women and children in the last stages of exhaustion. The alleys were littered with the corpses of the aged. The children were swollen from hunger. People collapsed in the streets. None had the strength to bury or even move the dead. Besides, there were too many to attend to. Some dug graves in their yards and lay down in them to wait for inevitable death. Some sat in the streets with their backs to the wall, gazing out at the Temple. They wanted the Holy Sanctuary to be the very last sight their eyes took in. Throughout this calamity, neither mourning nor moaning was heard. Hunger wasted away all human compassion; thirst dried up the tears of sorrow.

The Zealots, for the time being, were immune to the hunger. They had supplies, stolen and wrenched from the citizens. The Zealots could not tolerate the bodies lying in the streets. Not only was it demoralizing, but the stench was overpowering. At first, the Zealots piled the bodies in heaps and burned them. Later they resorted to throwing the corpses over the city wall into the Kidron Valley below.

The Roman camp was well supplied with fruit, grain and drink. Roman troops feasted in full view of the Jews atop the walls and roasted their food so the smell would carry into the city, adding to the Jews' torture. Some of the revolutionaries realized the futility of their hopes, for hunger had invaded their camp as well. They deserted to the Roman camps. A few Romans took pity on their swollen bodies and gave them food and water. Because their ravaged bodies were unused to normal quantities of food, their stomachs expanded and burst.

One of the Zealots was seen picking through his excrement, looking for coins and gems. Thereupon, several Roman mercenaries grabbed other Zealots, ripped open their bowels and began looking for coins. Two thousand Zealots were torn apart in this manner.

Not knowing whether to yield to hunger or risk being cut open while still alive, others defected. They were brought before Titus, and they told him tales of the horror that was befalling Jerusalem. Houses were being turned into mass graves. When a house became full of bodies, its doors were sealed and the next house was used. Men searched the sewers for scraps to eat. Women picked through the dunghills. What was once disgusting and repulsive became a precious morsel that might bring survival for perhaps one more day. In all, six hundred thousand had perished thus far.

As the days wore slowly on, the Zealots still maintained their hope of victory. The streets were so piled with bodies that no one could walk without trampling on them.

The Romans began cutting down trees to erect new rampworks against the Antonia Fortress. Jerusalem, which was once surrounded by great forests, was now bare. How desolate the Holy City sat, her beauty and glory gone.

The battering rams were hauled up the ramps. Yochanan ordered that the rampworks be set ablaze. The Zealots ran forth, but hunger and despair had taken their toll. They lacked resolve, determination and, most of all, hope. Their hands went limp, and their torches fell down to the ground.

Two Martyrs
25 Sivan, 70 c.e.

The two great luminaries of the Jewish nation, Rabban Shimon ben Gamliel the Prince and Rabbi Yishmael ben Elisha, the former High Priest, were captured.

"Yishmael, Yishmael," cried Rabban Shimon ben Gamliel. "We are being led to execution as though we had defiled the *Shabbos*, as though we had worshipped idols, as though we had succumbed to immorality, as though we were murderers."

"Were we perhaps not careful in taking care of the poor?" Rabbi Yishmael responded. "Did we perhaps not judge cases correctly? Did we concern ourselves with our own needs and neglect the widows and orphans?"

"Yishmael, you know it wasn't so," Rabban Shimon ben Gamliel answered.

"Still, we must accept our fate," the High Priest said in a muffled tone.

As they approached the executioner, Rabban Shimon ben Gamliel said, "The High Priest is greater than I. Let me be killed first."

"The Prince is greater than I," Rabbi Yishmael insisted. "Let me be killed first."

The executioner drew lots, and Rabban Shimon ben Gamliel was to be killed first. The executioner raised his sword and cut off the head of Rabban Shimon. Rabbi Yishmael bent and lifted the head of Rabban Shimon. He placed his eyes against the eyes of Rabban Shimon ben Gamliel and his mouth against the mouth of Rabban Shimon ben Gamliel.

"Holy lips, faithful lips," Rabbi Yishmael wept. "Lips that uttered pearls of wisdom now lick the dust." Rabbi Yishmael trembled and cried.

The executioner laughed. "Fool," he said. "Why do you cry over the death of your friend? Cry for yourself, for your death will be more cruel."

The daughter of Titus heard the moaning and came to see what was causing it. She saw Rabbi Yishmael. Never before had she seen so handsome a man. She begged her father to spare him so she could have him for herself. Titus rebuked the selfish request of his daughter and ordered that the execution proceed.

His daughter made one more request. "Then give me the skin of his head."

Titus granted this request and ordered that the executioner remove the flesh from Rabbi Yishmael's living head. When the executioner came to the place upon which the *tefillin* rested, the High Priest emitted a cry.

"For my life I do not cry, but for my *tefillin* I cry," he said.

The valiant manner in which these two sages accepted and met their deaths was admired by all who saw and heard of it. Even the heartless executioner could not hold back his tears. Titus' daughter had the skin of Rabbi Yishmael's head preserved in balsam and kept it in a glass jar by her bedside. Although Rabbi Yishmael's lips could no longer move, his death still spoke of his devotion to his Father in Heaven and to the Jewish nation.

ASSAULT ON THE ANTONIA FORTRESS
1 TAMMUZ, 70 C.E.

The Romans began their assault on the Antonia Fortress. With great determination, they battered the wall. But they had underestimated its strength, for the stones did not move or crack. Earlier, Yochanan had dug a tunnel from the Antonia under the original rampworks. This tunnel had caused the ramps to collapse. However, the tunnel also passed under the walls of the Antonia, and during the night that section of the fortress wall had collapsed.

The Romans were delighted at the Jews' miscalculation and proceeded to pour in through the breach. But Yochanan was a clever strategist; the end of the tunnel had been blocked by a thick wall. The Romans still had no entry into the fortress.

Two days later, Titus, sensing the frustration of his troops, asked for volunteers to climb the Antonia walls and assault the Jews from within. Though the mission seemed suicidal, twelve men volunteered. Bravely, they climbed up the walls while being assailed with stones and spears from the Jews above.

The Roman legions stood in awe, for until now, such feats of bravery were displayed only by the Zealots. Four of the men managed to get over the wall, but they were beaten by the Jews and killed. The remaining eight retreated to their camp, maimed and wounded.

ANTONIA CAPTURED
5 TAMMUZ, 70 C.E.

The night was still. The Romans and Jews were fast asleep. It was well past midnight. Twenty Roman sentries crept to the collapsed tunnel and squeezed in through a hole in Yochanan's wall. Quietly they made their way to the top of the fortress. They killed the Zealot guards as they slept. One of the Romans sounded the trumpet. The Zealots awoke and, upon hearing the trumpet, thought that all the Roman legions had made their way into the fortress. The Jews retreated into the complex adjacent to the Antonia, the Holy Temple.

Titus, also hearing the trumpet, ordered ladders to be set against the Antonia's walls. The Roman legionnaires ascended unchallenged. The Zealots' retreat into the Temple was slow. Many were still in the Antonia as the fortress filled with Romans. In the dark it was difficult to tell friend from foe.

The fighting was furious as the combatants were pressed

against one another. The battle lasted until the next afternoon. The Antonia was strewn with the battle victims. But it was the Romans who now held the fortress, and the remaining Jews retreated into the Lord's Sanctuary.

CHAPTER IV
THE BATTLE FOR THE TEMPLE

TITUS OFFERS PEACE
17 TAMMUZ, 70 C.E.

Titus had already moved his headquarters into the Antonia Fortress. Each day the combat centered around the wall that separated the Antonia from the Holy Temple. On the seventeenth day of *Tammuz*, the morning *tamid* sacrifice was not offered. The priests had all been called into battle. None remained in the Temple who did not suffer from a wound or blemish which made them unfit for the service. Nor could any sacrificial sheep be found. In the previous two centuries, the *tamid* sacrifice had been brought twice each day without fail, once in the morning and again in the afternoon. In all the days and years of war with Rome, the sacrificial rites had not been interrupted, even once— until this mournful day. The Jews took this to be a bad omen indeed.

Titus, upon hearing of the Jews' dilemma, offered to make peace with them and restore the sacrificial rites if they would surrender and promise allegiance to Rome. Many of the priests did defect. They did not know whether or not Titus would keep his pledge, but remaining in the Temple, knowing the Temple service could not be performed, was unbearable. The defectors were sent to seek refuge in Gophna, twelve miles north of the Holy City, so that they would not have to bear witness to the terrible events about to unfold.

FIGHTING IN THE TEMPLE
22 TAMMUZ, 70 C.E.

Surrounding the inner Temple Courtyard was a low fence. Stone markers were placed at intervals with Greek and Latin writing carved on them reading, "Let no foreigner nor anyone defiled pass beyond this point under penalty of death." But, alas, defilement had indeed passed beyond the fence and its markers. The inner precincts and the sacred area had become littered with the bodies of fallen Jews, and the stubbornness of the Zealots was now en-

An ancient plaque that stood outside the Temple Courtyard. It is written in Greek and warns that any gentile that passes beyond this point is subject to the death penalty.

ticing the foreigners to enter.

Titus chose his most valiant soldiers and officers and ordered them to storm the Temple grounds at three o'clock in the morning when the Zealot guards were sure to be fast asleep. However, the guards were awake, and as the Romans poured into the sacred area, the Jews sounded the alarm. Great confusion broke out. In the darkness, the combatants began to kill one another, unable to distinguish between friend and foe. Realizing the dilemma, the Zealots and the Romans ceased their fighting and maintained their positions until the morning.

When daybreak came, the combatants renewed their fight with vigor. The Romans fought bravely, for Titus was watching from one of the towers in the Antonia Fortress. Every Roman wanted to please his venerated commander-in-chief. The

A Roman spear found in the remains of a Second Temple Era house. A clay weight with the name of the priestly clan Bar Katros engraved on it was also discovered in these remains. The arm of a woman was found nearby.

Jews, likewise, fought valiantly. They were fighting for their very lives and for their Holy Temple.

The battleground was confined. It was like fighting in the arena of a theater. Titus and Roman soldiers stood watching from the Antonia, cheering their forces on. The Jews, who stood in the rear of the battle area, cheered the Zealots on. It was like a nightmarish, staged play. After fighting for eight hours, no decisive victory could be claimed, so the Romans withdrew into the Antonia.

That very day, at five o'clock in the afternoon, the Jews launched a surprise attack on the Mount of Olives where the tenth legion had remained to serve as reinforcements. Though the tenth legion was not prepared for the raid, neither were they as battle-worn as the Jews were. A short skirmish ensued, and the Jews pulled back into the Temple.

TEMPLE PORTICO ABLAZE
24 , 70 C.E.

Surrounding the inside walls of the Temple was a line of marble columns. These columns ran parallel to the wall, about forty-five feet from the wall. These forty-foot high columns supported a wooden roof that extended from the top of the columns to the Temple wall. This was called the Temple portico. The building adjacent to the Temple in the north was the Antonia Fortress. The Antonia and the Temple shared a common wall. The length of the Antonia Fortress ran along the northern Temple wall. In the four corners of the fortress were great towers, each eighty-two

The ancient remains of a cistern built by Shimon Hatzaddik, circa 300 b.c.e. It was built against the Northern Temple Wall which is to the left in the photograph. It was called Bereichas Yisrael, Israelite Pool. The two water tunnels in the photo are filled with trash and debris. They have never been explored.

feet high. The southeastern tower was one hundred and fifteen feet high. The Zealots feared that the Romans, who had possession of the Antonia, would ascend the southwestern tower and lower themselves onto the roof of the portico, which was about thirty-five feet below the top of the tower. They did not concern themselves with the southeastern tower of the Antonia as it was seventy feet above the top of the portico roof.

The Jews decided to pull down the portico at the northwest corner. Thirty feet of its length was demolished, and the wooden roof was set ablaze. These Jews first set fire to the Holy Temple. The Romans, seeing that the Jews were burning down their own refuge, threw torches to keep the portico ablaze. The Jews allowed the fire to spread along the northern portico, which helped serve their purpose.

At that time, a Jew named Yonassan walked outside the western city gate toward the Roman camp. Alone, he walked with confidence and defiance, taunting and challenging any Roman to come and fight him. The Romans took him to be a fool and were reluctant to accept his challenge. What glory could there be in the death of a fool? Who would be willing to risk his reputation or his life to fight Yonassan? When Yonassan's taunts were ignored by the Romans, he called them cowards and weaklings.

One Roman, Pudens by name, could bear the tormenting indignities no longer. He donned his battle regalia and ran down to meet the Jew in mortal combat. As fate would have it, Pudens stumbled and fell before Yonassan, who pulled out a dagger and slit the Roman's throat. He laid his foot on the body of the slain warrior and held up the dagger, still dripping with blood, for all the Romans to see. One of the Roman archers who was watching from the camp above drew back the string of his bow, took careful aim and released the arrow. It found its mark in the chest of Yonassan. Slowly, he fell to the ground, writhing in agony.

COMPASSIONATE MOTHER
27 TAMMUZ, 70 C.E.

From their base in the Antonia Fortress, the Romans

managed to invade the outer Temple Courtyard. The Jews retreated to the inner courtyard, and the Romans secured their position. The Romans began to raise up four ramps against the inner Temple walls, two in the north and two in the west. They planned to ascend the ramps to the roof of the inner portico, for the inner courtyard was also surrounded by a portico. From the roof of the western portico, the Romans hoped to gain access into the Temple. The Jews placed dry grasses, tinder and pitch under the roof of the western portico and withdrew. The roof of the western portico was soon crowded with Roman troops. The Jews flung torches into the combustible mass under the roof. Within moments, the portico was ablaze.

Some Roman soldiers jumped back from the top of the Temple wall to the outer courtyard below, falling thirty feet to the ground. Others jumped forward into the Zealots' midst and were slain. Some soldiers, who were surrounded by the flames, impaled themselves on their own swords in order to escape the more painful death of being burned alive. Many, however, were indeed burned alive. In the end, all those Romans who had stood on the roof of the western portico perished, except for one.

One Roman, Artorius by name, stood on top of the blazing roof and called to his tentmate Lucius, who was standing below. "Dearest Lucius, catch me when I jump, and you will inherit all that is mine."

Artorius jumped onto Lucius and survived, but Lucius was killed by the impact. It was as though the number of Romans to perish that day was divinely decreed.

Those Jews not engaged in the fighting roamed the

streets of the city within the innermost wall, which still had not been breached. Hunger was taking its toll. Women were scraping at the dust in the street for a crumb to eat. Men gnawed at their belts and shoes. Strands of straw became a feast.

There was a woman, Miriam, daughter of Eliezer, from a most distinguished and wealthy family that had fled to Jerusalem. Her riches had been seized by the greedy Zealots, and she was now reduced to begging for food for herself and her infant son. Often, she begged strangers to have mercy upon her and slay her, but no one obliged the wishes of the hunger-crazed woman. Her body had worn thin, and her bones were unable to carry the weight of her skin.

She grabbed her infant and cried out, "Poor baby! Why should I keep you alive? What hope is there for you? For what shall we pray? If hunger is victorious, we shall perish. If the Romans are victorious, we shall be enslaved. If the Zealots are victorious, that would be an even crueler fate. Come, my son, be my food. Keep your dear mother alive, for there is no hope for you."

She killed her son, roasted the flesh and ate half of it. The odor of roasting flesh spread into the streets. Some Jews, smelling the odor, burst in through her door.

"What delicacies are you hiding?" they demanded.

She produced the half-eaten body of her son. They recoiled in horror.

"Why are you so repulsed?" she inquired. "Are you more compassionate than a tender-hearted mother? I have eaten; why do you not wish to partake? If you do not want to eat of my sacrifice, then leave it for me."

The sad story was told over and over in the streets. How low the nation of the Lord had fallen.

THE WALL STILL STANDS
2 AV, 70 C.E.

Titus ordered the battering rams to be brought and placed against the inner western Temple wall. The Temple walls had been built by the master builder Herod, the king of Judea a hundred years earlier.

The rarely seen northern section of the Western Wall. It has been nicknamed the "Kossel Katan," or small wall. The Romans attempted an assault against the Temple at this point.

The stones were about four feet thick and four feet high, and their lengths varied. Each stone weighed between two tons and four hundred tons. For six days, the rams battered furiously, but the war machines made no impact on the wall.

THE TEMPLE GATES BURNED
8 AV, 70 C.E.

When Titus realized that the battering rams were of no use against the sanctuary, a different ploy was tried. Ladders were raised against the huge walls, and scores of Romans ascended the ladders. But the Jews mounted the top of the wall and pushed the ladders back with the legionnaires still on them. Many Romans were hurled to their deaths.

Meanwhile, other Romans were setting fire to the gates of the Temple. These gates, which were plated and intricately designed with silver, had been sealed shut by the Zealots. The fires melted the silver, and soon the inner wooden structure gave way.

The Romans dashed in and tossed torches onto the roof of the portico that still remained. The roof was set ablaze, and the Jews trapped inside the Temple court were surrounded by flames. The fire continued to burn long into the night, when finally the entire portico collapsed in a thunderous roar.

THE TEMPLE CAPTURED
9 AV, 70 C.E.

A false prophet arose among the people and declared that the masses should assemble in the Temple, for on that very day, the Lord, in all His honor and glory, was going to deliver His nation from their distress. Desperate men are willing to believe anything in times of despair, and many fled into the inner Temple courts.

In the years preceding, great omens had been seen. One night, a star appeared in the shape of a sword and hung suspended above the city for an entire year. The false prophets claimed that this was a sign that the Lord would slay the Roman invaders. But the Sages said that it was an omen that bore evil tidings for the Jewish people.

One Passover eve, at three o'clock in the morning, another star appeared that illuminated the night sky for half an hour. The charlatans interpreted this to mean that the darkness caused by the Romans would soon be dispersed. The Sages said that the great hope of the Jewish people would quickly fade into the great darkness. That same Passover, a cow, brought by one festival pilgrim for a sacrifice, gave birth to what appeared to be a lamb. The false prophets said the fate of Israel would supernaturally change for the better.

"Is a lamb greater than a cow?" the wise men asked. "Israel's fortune will not take a turn for the better."

During that same festival, two great bronze doors of the inner court, which normally required twenty men to open, opened on their own. The deceivers claimed that the Lord was opening the doors of His Heart. The Sages said that the doors of the Temple were opening to the Romans.

On the twenty-sixth day of *Iyar* of that year, a most amazing phenomenon appeared. Before sunset on that day, everyone in Jerusalem saw images of chariots moving through the sky and encircling the city. The false prophets and the Sages argued as to what it meant. On the feast of *Sukkos*, a violent commotion arose in the Temple at night, and ghastly voices were heard saying, "We are leaving this place." Once again, there were conflicting interpretations.

On this very day, the ninth day of *Av*, the false prophets were promising deliverance, and the Sages were bemoaning the doom. On this very day, the truth would be known.

Titus assembled his legions to invade the Temple through the burning gateways. Leading the Roman legionnaires into battle was Tiberius Alexander, a renegade Jew. Tiberius' father Alexander was a noble and respected Jew who gave generously of his wealth to beautify the magnificent Eastern Gate of the Temple Court. As misfortune would have it, Alexander's son was now leading the Roman assault against that very gate. When the Heavenly decrees turn against the children of Israel, every bit of twisted irony and misfortune is hurled against them.

The Romans now occupied the outer courtyard of the Temple. The Jews ran from the inner courtyard to badger and intimidate the Romans. From eight o'clock in the morning until eleven, the raids continued. The Romans, though frightened by the fanatical zeal of the Jews, did not yield. The weary Jews retired to the sacred inner precincts and sealed the doors.

Titus convened a council in the Antonia to discuss an invasion into the most sacred area. The plan was to invade at dawn the following morning, as it was already drawing close to evening.

A runner broke into the council meeting. The inner Temple was on fire! In a state of confusion, everyone ran out to see. Almost every Roman was carrying a torch, for by now, it was dark. The Romans took their torches and threw them over the innermost wall of the Temple to add to the conflagration. The flames soared upward.

The Jews trapped inside huddled around the Altar. Spears and arrows were flung inside the courts. The bodies of the Jews were heaped in mounds around the place of atonement. Some were slain, others were overcome by smoke, and still others were crushed in the nighttime panic. A stream of blood ran across the Temple floor and flowed down the eastern steps.

Later that evening, Titus, drunk with victory, brought a harlot into the Holy of Holies. He spread out a Torah scroll and committed a blasphemous sin upon it. Titus then took his sword and slashed the curtain. Miraculously, the curtain began to bleed, whereupon Titus shouted, "I have killed Him. I have killed the Lord of Israel."

This tragedy of the Jewish nation happened on the ninth day of the month of *Av*. It was the very same month and the very same day, four hundred and ninety years earlier, that the First Temple was set ablaze by King Nebuchadnezzar, the Babylonian tyrant, when he destroyed the city of Jerusalem and left it in ruins. (*See photograph on following page.*)

The remains of a First Temple era house destroyed by Nebuchadnezzar

WOE TO ME
10 AV, 70 C.E.

While the Temple continued to burn into the next day, the attackers plundered it. The surviving Jews were slaughtered. There was no pity for women or children. Priests and laymen alike were butchered. No part of the Temple floor could be seen because of the multitude of bodies. Through the roar of the flames and the falling walls, the cries of the victims were heard.

Some Jews huddled in a great mass in a corner where the portico had stood. The Romans burned them alive. Some of the priests climbed to the roof of the Sanctuary. Atop the wall that surrounded the roof were long metal spikes, placed there to deter birds from alighting on the Sanctuary wall. The spikes were ripped from the wall and hurled by the priests at the Romans below. But the flames leaped upward toward the roof. The entire city seemed to be ablaze. Cries of pain, shrieks of terror and moans of mourning were heard everywhere. The surrounding hills echoed the din within the city.

Several years before, a Jew named Yehoshua ben Chanan had come to the Temple courts during the feast of *Sukkos*. With a wild glint in his eyes, he had screamed out, "A voice from the east, a voice from the west, a voice from the four directions, a voice against Jerusalem and her Temple. A voice against the bride, a voice against the groom, a voice against the assembled. Woe, woe to Jerusalem."

Day and night, he continued to speak in a strange voice. He muttered while wandering the streets and alleys, "Woe, woe to Jerusalem." Some of the citizens became angry at the man and beat him savagely. But he did not stop ranting, "Woe, woe to Jerusalem." He was brought before the Roman governor, for it was believed that he was possessed by some evil spirit. He was whipped and tortured in order to drive out the demon. He neither begged for mercy nor shed a tear. When the magistrate asked his name, he merely replied, "Woe, woe to Jerusalem."

In the end, he was judged insane and released. He continued to wander the streets, and still he continued his mournful cry, "Woe, woe to Jerusalem." He never cursed those who continually taunted and abused him. Every festival, when Jews from all over the land gathered in the Holy City, they all heard his soulful lament. And so, for seven years and five months, he continued. He was still wandering about, calling out, "Woe, woe to Jerusalem," when a stone, hurled from a Roman catapult, struck him. As he lay dying upon the ground, he moaned, "Woe, woe to Jerusalem. And now, woe to me."

Chapter V
Jerusalem in Ruins

Gladness into Mourning
15 Av, 70 c.e.

Fire still raged in the Temple Courtyard. The Zealots fled to the Upper and Lower Cities, the only protected sections of the Holy City that remained. The Romans brought their standards and flags into the Temple grounds and posted them near the eastern gate. The legionnaires still encamped on the Mount of Olives, across from the eastern gate, watched with relief and pride.

The Romans raided the Temple treasuries, which were so laden with precious metals that the price of gold soon dropped by one half throughout the Middle East. Some priests were found hiding in the Temple grounds. They were brought before Titus and executed.

The last remaining wall of the city began at the south-eastern corner of the Temple. It went southward, following the contour of the Kidron Valley. It then turned west as far as the Valley of Hennom. From there it began its northern course up to the Tower of David. From that fortress it turned to the east and went across the mountain where the Upper City was located. The wall crossed the mountain and then cut across the Tyropean Valley until it joined the western Temple wall. This area was the last secure confine of Jerusalem.

The surviving revolutionaries and citizens were crowded into this district. Titus stood atop the western Temple wall and addressed Yochanan and Shimon and their revolutionary cohorts standing below.

"The leaders of the rebellion must surrender," Titus declared. "They will be justly punished, but their followers will be granted immunity."

Yochanan demanded that they all be granted safe passage out of the war-torn city into the Judean hills. Titus was appalled that the Zealots tried to impose demands as though they were the victors instead of the prisoners. Titus ordered his troops to devastate the city.

Before this dreadful war, this very day, the fifteenth of *Av*, was a holiday. It was a day of celebration. The cutting of the trees for the Temple firewood had been completed. Maidens would dance in the vineyards in all their linen finery. They would all wear borrowed clothing in order not to embarrass those who did not have the proper garments. Matchmakers would make matches, and not long after, the music of betrothal celebrations would fill the land. But now there was no dancing. There was no celebration. There was no music. The Temple had been destroyed; Judea had been desolated. The survivors of the Jewish nation were surrounded in the last remaining corner of Jerusalem. The enemy was making demands. Starvation devastated the city. This day was no longer a day of feasts and gaiety; it was a day of mourning and despair.

TOWER OF DAVID
16 AV, 70 C.E.

Near the junction of the inner city wall and the western Temple wall was the city archives building. All documents pertaining to domestic life in the Holy City were stored there. The Romans set fire to this municipal building and destroyed it. When a city's documents are destroyed, its link to the past is severed. Hope for the future is inextricably linked to the promises of the past. That link was broken.

The Romans had also set fire to the Lower City, southwest of the Temple. The town council was destroyed along with the elegant homes and mansions of the district. The fire spread to the Palace of Queen Helena, where her descendants still lived. Driven from their royal abode, they surrendered to the Romans. These descendants of the noble Helena were bound in chains and taken to Rome.

The Zealots ran toward the old Herodian Palace which stood next to the Tower of David. The Palace grounds were one thousand feet long and two hundred feet wide. Fifty-foot high walls protected this royal fortress. Two great mansions stood at the northern and southern ends of the complex, capable of housing thousands of guests. Between

Southern Temple Wall, showing the steps that led up to the southern gateways.

these structures was a royal park with paths and fountains. In times of peace, tame doves hovered over the magnificent orchards. Now, the trees were bare, and the doves had long since departed.

Eight thousand four hundred Jews had sought shelter there. Yochanan and Shimon assumed that they planned to surrender, so they had them slaughtered. Two Romans were also captured. One was slain and his body dragged through the broken city streets. The other was bound and brought to the western Temple wall so that the Romans could witness his execution. Miraculously, the prisoner untied the bindings on his hands and escaped. He made his way to his Roman compatriots and was brought before

Titus. Titus stripped him of his rank and dismissed him from the legion for having been captured; to a Roman soldier, humiliation was worse than death.

RETREAT INTO THE SEWERS
17 AV, 70 C.E.

The remainder of the Lower City was burned, all the way to the southern city wall by the Shiloach Brook. There were no captives or wealth to be taken. All the people had

The remains of the ancient sewer that ran under ancient Jerusalem. This was the last refuge of the desperate Zealots.

fled to the Upper City.

In former times, during the festival of *Sukkos*, water was drawn from the Shiloach Brook and brought through the southern Temple gates. The water was poured on the Altar with much pomp and gaiety. It was said that "whoever did not witness the Drawing of the Water has never witnessed celebration in his life." Now it could be said that whoever did not witness the destruction of Jerusalem has never witnessed devastation in his life.

Some of the citizens who were too weak from hunger did not flee to the Upper City across from the western Temple wall. They wandered out the city gates into the hands of the Romans. These unfortunate citizens were butchered and fed to the dogs that accompanied the Roman soldiers.

Shimon and Yochanan now devised one last plan. The Upper City contained many underground vaults. These vaults served as drainage conduits for the rainwater. They carried the precious water from under the streets into the main vault running under the Tyropean Valley. From there, the water was conducted to cisterns and pools at the base of the Lower City. Yochanan and Shimon decided that everyone should take whatever food they had managed to steal into these vaults. They would allow the Romans to capture the Upper City. The foreign invaders, after realizing that the destroyed Jerusalem had proved to be a most inhospitable home, would depart. The Jews would then resurface from the sewers and rebuild the city. This was the desperate plan of desperate men.

Titus ordered his legionnaires to build two rampworks. One was to be built west of the Herodian Palace. The second was to be raised north of where the council building had stood. The Upper City would be invaded from these two points. Some of the Edomites, who still remained in the city, foresaw the futility of the Zealot plan. They sent emissaries to Titus to obtain a guarantee of immunity. Shimon was told of the plot and executed the Edomite captains. The Edomite soldiers were kept under careful scrutiny.

In spite of the Zealots' watchful eyes, forty thousand Jews managed to surrender to the Romans. So many of them were taken as slaves that the price of Jewish slaves fell below the price of cattle. During that time, two priests also defected. One, whose name was Yehoshua, gave Titus two golden lampstands and other treasures from the sacred Temple, including gold bowls and plates. He also gave the commander-in-chief the holy garments of the High Priest, set with precious stones. The other priest, Pinchas, a Temple treasurer, gave Titus many priestly garments and a supply of scarlet and purple wool, together with herbs and spices that were used for the Temple incense. They surrendered many other treasures and ornaments. The two priests were granted their freedom.

The remains of the king's palace in the Fortress of David. This was the site of the last stronghold of the Zealots in Jerusalem.

ROMAN FLAG IN THE FORTRESS OF DAVID
7 ELUL, 70 C.E.

On the seventh day of *Elul*, the Romans broke through the western city wall near the Herodian Palace. For the most part, the city was empty of life. The Romans brought their flags and standards to the three towers of the Fortress of David. This fortress, once thought by all to be impregnable, was now in Roman hands.

The remaining survivors of a once noble nation were hiding in the sewers below. Like vermin, they groped their way through the sewage toward the Shiloach Brook.

The Romans staged a celebration atop the towers, amazed that they had concluded the capture of the city without a fight. They ran through the streets looking for survivors. Those who were too weak to find their way into the sewers below were captured. Homes were set ablaze; abandoned fortunes were confiscated. In the course of the raids, the Romans entered houses looking for booty and, to their horror, found whole families, dead from starvation. Rooms were filled with victims of the ravages of hunger. The alleyways were choked with corpses, the streets littered with bodies. Fires were quenched by the blood of the fallen.

DEATH IN THE TEMPLE COURTYARD
8 ELUL, 70 C.E.

Titus entered Jerusalem. He marveled at the Tower of David which was now in his hands. The Zealots had used this fortress as a prison for those who had opposed their revolutionary tactics. The prisoners were kept in the fortress by the Romans until Titus arrived. The commander-in-chief now released them. He ordered his troops to destroy what remained of Jerusalem, but the Tower of David was to be left unharmed. It would serve as a memorial to the might of Jerusalem which he had conquered.

The remaining survivors found wandering the streets were herded into the Women's Courtyard on the destroyed Temple Mount. A Jew-hating Roman named Fronto was placed in charge of deciding their fate.

Fronto had many Jews executed. Some were bound in chains and sent to Rome as part of the captured spoils, while others were sold into slavery and sent to Egypt. Their forefathers had been slaves on the cruel and harsh sands along the Nile, and now the new slaves were joined in bondage with their ancestors' memory. Some survivors were kept alive to fight wild beasts in arenas as a sport for the Roman spectators. Fronto was so slow in deciding the fate of so many that eleven thousand Jews perished of starvation in the Women's Courtyard.

As the soldiers began to tear up the streets of Jerusalem, they discovered the underground vaults. Two thousand dead bodies were found obstructing these narrow sewers, blocking the Zealots' advance to the south and safety. A few Zealots were found alive, Yochanan and Shimon among them. These once powerful and robust tyrants were now drawn and thin from starvation. They were sent to Rome, where Shimon was beheaded and Yochanan died in prison.

The capture of Judea had been completed. In the Holy City alone, the number of those who died during the brutal war and from the ravages of hunger was one million one hundred thousand. The number of captives was ninety-seven thousand.

CHAPTER VI
AFTERMATH

JERUSALEM IN RUINS
70 C.E.

The Holy Temple was destroyed. Jerusalem was in ruins. Rome had complete dominion over Judea. The defeated Jews were permitted to stay in the land of their ancestors, where they remained faithful to the Lord who had vented His burning anger against the stones of Zion and His Holy Temple.

The triumphant Roman general Titus and his warriors were intoxicated with their victory. They plundered the land, seizing the homes and possessions of the Jews.

"Whoever does not kill a Jew shall be killed," decreed Titus.

As the rage of revenge subsided, Titus declared, "Whoever kills a Jew must pay a fine of forty *zuz*."

Roman coins proclaiming Judea
Capta, Judea is captured

Titus riding his chariot in the victory
parade in Rome to celebrate the downfall of Judea

When the fear of the Romans was firmly instilled in the
Jews, Titus declared, "Whoever kills a Jew will be killed."
(*Gittin* 55b)

A special tax was placed upon all the Jews in the Roman
Empire. The Fiscus Judaici (Jew tax) was to be fifteen *shekel*s
each year, in addition to the taxes placed on all citizens of
the empire.

"Those who did not wish to pay the tax to the Temple
treasury," lamented Rabban Yochanan ben Zakai, "must
now pay the tax to their enemy. Those who refused to give
the half-*shekel* are now compelled to give fifteen full *shekel*s.
Those who did not repair the streets and roads for the
festival pilgrims are forced to make repairs for the emperor's
attendants." (*Mechilta Shemos* 19:1)

The downtrodden Jews lamented the great misfortune
that had befallen them, not realizing that the great horror
of exile had not yet come.

Titus Flavius marched with his troops across the desert into Egypt. From there he set sail back to Rome to celebrate his victory in Judea. He brought with him the Jewish Zealot leaders and seven hundred rebels, men of outstanding stature and physique, to put on display back home.

Titus was greeted by his father, the emperor Vespasian, and great masses of Romans who also came to meet the conquering hero. A day was chosen for a victory celebration. The night before the eventful day, all the soldiers marched to the Temple of Isis where Vespasian and his sons Titus and Domitian slept the night.

At dawn, all Romans gathered in the streets. A great dais with ivory chairs had been arranged in front of the temple. As the emperor and his sons sat down, great cheers went up from the soldiers and the attending crowd. After the emperor's short speech, the soldiers were invited to partake in a royal feast and to watch the victory parade.

Each participant in the parade carried some of the spoils from Judea. It was like a flowing river of jubilant humanity. Gold and silver, gems and works of art were borne high. Wild beasts decorated with circus trappings added a bizarre atmosphere to the spectacle.

Great horse-drawn stages, bearing scenes of the Judean war, passed the cheering crowd. The stages were decorated with gold embroidered tapestries. One stage depicted a scene of battle, another showed prisoners being led off to captivity. There were city walls with defenders on top and Roman soldiers overwhelming them; blood was pouring down the walls. One stage portrayed a sea battle, another a devastated town. Some of the stages were three and four stories high. The crowd was in awe, fearing that the huge stages would topple and spill their war scenes into the streets.

The most prominent stage bore the spoils taken from the Jewish Temple. A golden candelabra, a golden table and the most prized of the spoils, a Torah scroll.

The parade ended at the temple of Jupiter Capitoline. The Zealot leader, Shimon ben Giora, was brought to the steps of the temple. Vespasian gave the order, and Shimon was executed. The crowd cheered victoriously.

The fight for Jerusalem had ended thousands of miles away from the devastated city, on the steps of the temple of Jupiter in Rome. Sixty-five years later, the final chapter of the struggle for Judea would end, once again, on the steps of a temple of Jupiter.

RABBAN YOCHANAN BEN ZAKAI
THE LIGHT OF ISRAEL

With Jerusalem in ashes, Yavneh became the religious center in Judea. The head of the *Sanhedrin* was the aged Rabban Yochanan ben Zakai. Years earlier, Rabban Yochanan ben Zakai had predicted to Vespasian that the illustrious Roman would be chosen as the next emperor of Rome. In recognition of the sage's prophetic ability, Vespasian had granted Rabban Yochanan ben Zakai's wish that the city of Yavneh and the descendants of Hillel the

Prince be spared Rome's revenge.

Because of Rabban Yochanan ben Zakai's intercession, Torah flourished in Yavneh, but the Jews still mourned for Jerusalem and her Temple. Even after the Temple Mount was laid to waste, they continued to visit her three times a year as in years past. (*Shir Hashirim Rabah* 8:9) Once, Rabban Yochanan ben Zakai was walking in Jerusalem with his student Rabbi Yehoshua ben Chananiah. "Woe to us," moaned Rabbi Yehoshua, "for we have lost the Altar, our place of atonement." (*Avos d'Rabbi Nassan* 4:5)

Rabban Yochanan ben Zakai corrected his student. "We still have an act for atonement that equals the Altar, deeds of kindness."

Rabban Yochanan ben Zakai established schools and houses of prayer in Yavneh. The greatest Sages taught and studied in the new religious center. Had it not been for Rabban Yochanan ben Zakai's foresight, the destruction of the Temple would have signaled the onset of the darkness of Torah. No wonder our Elders have called Rabban Yochanan ben Zakai "the Light of Israel." (*Berachos* 28b)

Rabban Yochanan ben Zakai died less than six years after Yavneh was established, less than five years after the Temple was destroyed. "The radiance of wisdom was gone forever." (*Sotah* 49a)

MASADA AND THE END OF THE FIRST REVOLT
73 C.E.

While the sages of Yavneh were concerning themselves

Masada

A TIME TO WEEP

with the restructuring of religious life and law, a band of unyielding Jewish Zealots still sought to defeat the Roman invaders. These Zealots, numbering less than one thousand men, women and children, took refuge in the Judean desert atop the mountain fortress of Masada.

The Masada Fortress was built one hundred years earlier by the Judean tyrant Herod the Great. He constructed the fort atop a fourteen-hundred-foot high plateau in the Judean Desert. It was graced with palaces and lavish bathhouses. It had several *mikvaos* and a synagogue. There were hundreds of rooms for storage and quarters for soldiers. The most fertile soil had been imported, and fields to cultivate crops were em-bedded on top of the plateau. A twenty-five-foot high wall enclosed the summit. Built into the four-thousand-two-hundred foot long wall were thirty-seven towers, each seventy feet in height. The palace had four towers, each ninety feet high, with a commanding view of the desert. Royal splendor contrasted with the barren desert sands. This was the setting

Clay lot with the name Ben Yair written on it, discovered in one of the rooms atop Masada

for the last stand of the Jewish revolutionaries.

The Zealots sent out raiding parties during the day and night, making the Romans' victory in Jerusalem difficult for them to savor. Earlier, when the Jews had still occupied

Jerusalem, these Zealots would raid the holy city and plunder Jewish homes in order to build up the stores and supplies. The Zealots had invaded Jerusalem and began a reign of terror. Suspected Roman sympathizers and pacifists were murdered.

These radicals had split into rival factions, each burning the storehouses of the other. Because of their reckless deeds, hundreds of thousands of Jews starved to death during the Roman siege of Jerusalem. The Zealots brought more havoc and destruction upon their fellow Jews than did the Romans. On the first day of Passover, the anniversary of our nation's freedom, the neighboring Jewish town of Ein Gedi was decimated and its spoils brought back to Masada.

Before the Roman conquest, the Zealots, including all the rival factions, numbered about twenty-three thousand men. Now, seven years later, nine hundred and sixty-seven remained, including women and children. The leader of these Zealots was Elazar ben Yair. The Roman governor of Jerusalem, Flavius Silva, personally led the assault against Masada.

Silva brought ten thousand of the ablest troops of the infamous Tenth Legion. Accompanying them were thousands of Jewish slaves who had been captured in the Holy City. Silva had a siege wall constructed around the base of the mountain. A three-hundred-foot high earthen ramp was built against the western side of Masada. A seventy-five-foot wide stone road was paved on top, and the Roman war machines were rolled in place.

Battering rams pounded mercilessly at the wall on top.

Stones and flaming torches were shot into the fortress, keeping the Zealots at bay. The western fortress wall was breached, but the defenders had managed to block the opening with great wooden beams, reinforced with mounds of earth. Silva ordered his men to burn the wooden barrier down. The beams quickly caught fire and a great wall of flames rose upward. Suddenly, a wind came and blew the fire in the direction of the Romans, forcing them to retreat.

"Providence is on our side," proclaimed the Jewish defenders.

But just as suddenly, the wind changed course, and now it was the Romans who boasted of being on the side of Providence. As the barrier burned down, night fell and the Romans withdrew to their camp. The final assault against Masada would take place the next morning.

Elazar ben Yair, realizing that defeat was imminent, delivered an inspiring oration urging the defenders to commit mass suicide rather than accept defeat. Ten men were to be chosen by lots to slay the men, women and children. These ten survivors would then draw lots to choose one to kill the other nine and then to kill himself.

Elazar's speech to this remnant band of tired and worn revolutionaries is one of the great works of oratory of all time.

> "It is evident that tomorrow we will be captured, but now we are free to choose an honorable death together with our loved ones. Perhaps from the very outset, when we had our eyes set on freedom, and dealt harsh treatment upon our fellow Jews, we should have realized the Lord's will that His beloved were doomed. Did we really think after the Holy

City was burned to the ground that we alone would come through in safety, as though we were guiltless before the Lord, we who had been the teachers of all the others?

"Not even this impregnable fortress could save us, for the Lord has deprived us of all hope. This is His vengeance for the many sins we inflicted upon our countrymen in our time of madness. Let us pay the penalty, but not to our bitter foes, rather to the Lord, by our very own hands.

"Let our wives die without being dishonored. Let our children perish without knowing slavery. This shall be our monument to liberty. Let us destroy all our belongings and the fortress, but spare only one thing, our store of food. It will testify after our death that we did not die of want, but rather because of our determination to choose death over slavery."

During the darkness of that final night, the fortress was set ablaze. Loved ones embraced for the last time. The suicide pact was then carried out.

The next morning, the Romans rushed to the summit of Masada. They expected to be greeted by an assault from the Zealots. Instead, they found an eerie silence and smoke rising from the remaining embers.

Two Jewish women and five children, who had hidden in a cistern to avoid being killed, emerged and told the Romans what had transpired. The Romans found it difficult to believe their story, but soon they came upon the mass of slain bodies. Rather than joyously celebrate their victory, the Romans withdrew in sadness and admiration.

Masada marked the end of the First Revolt against Rome. The fall of Masada occurred on the first day of Passover, the anniversary of our nation's freedom.

ROMAN RULE CONTINUES
75-81 C.E.

Upon the death of Rabban Yochanan ben Zakai in 75 c.e., Rabban Gamliel II, known as Rabban Gamliel of Yavneh, was appointed head of the Jewish community. The revolutionary Zealots no longer threatened Rome or the Jewish people. Judea was in a state of subdued tranquility.

The Roman emperor Vespasian died in 79 c.e., nine years after Jerusalem was captured. He had the distinction of being the first Roman emperor to die a natural death. Vespasian was succeeded by his son Titus Flavius, the conqueror of Jerusalem. Titus was well educated and had accompanied his father on many military campaigns. When his father was appointed emperor, Titus had taken over the reigns of the Judean campaign. The Roman legions admired Titus' martial abilities, and the Senate appreciated his dispassion and fair-mindedness.

During Titus' short two-and-a-half year reign, Rome was beset by three great tragedies: the volcanic eruption of Mount Vesuvius, the great fire in Rome and an outbreak of bubonic plague. Titus earned the respect of his countrymen when he emptied the treasuries of Rome to alleviate the public's suffering from these misfortunes and tragedies. In Rome, Titus had but one enemy, his younger brother Domitian. Domitian had his eyes set on the emperor's throne. Titus, not trusting his younger brother, never gave him any position of power or influence.

Some suspected that Titus regretted his terrible role in the destruction of Jerusalem and the Temple. Rabban

Gamliel, together with Rabbi Eliezer and Rabbi Yehoshua, undertook a voyage to Rome. They sought to intercede on behalf of their people against the abuses of the Roman governors in Judea.

In Rome, the Sages saw the Jewish captives who yearned to be returned to their homeland. They watched young Jewish children playing in the streets with mounds of earth, pretending they were piles of grain. "This much must be set aside for the *terumah* tithe, and this much must be set aside for the *maaser* tithe," the children said. (*Yerushalmi Sanhedrin* 7:13)

Rabbi Yehoshua discovered the scholar Rabbi Yishmael ben Elisha in a Roman dungeon and raised a large sum of money to free him. (*Gittin* 58a)

Titus died suddenly at the age of forty in 81 c.e. His younger brother and rival, Domitian, was chosen by the Senate as the next emperor. Though he was only thirty years old, Domitian was already widely despised. During his fifteen-year reign, this tyrant murdered his political foes and mistrusted his few allies.

Domitian had an arch built in the Roman Forum. It commemorated his brother's defeat of Judea. It is called the Arch of Titus. Depicted inside were Roman soldiers carrying off the spoils from the Temple in Jerusalem. The warriors bearing the sacred *menorah* has come to personify the exile of the Jews. To this very day, Jews do not walk through the arch.

Domitian decreed many laws forbidding the practice of Judaism. Rabban Gamliel, Rabbi Eliezer and Rabbi Yehoshua returned to Rome to plead for mercy and a return of

above: The Arch of Titus
top left: Romans carrying off Menorah,
as depicted inside the Arch of Titus

above: Domitian

tolerance. As the Sages arrived, the Senate passed a law that was to take effect in thirty days, banning the presence of Jews throughout the Roman Empire. Though the Jewish nation was oppressed and murdered by those who sought to annihilate them, one in every ten citizens of the Roman Empire was Jewish. Like their ancestors in Egypt, the more the oppressor sought to destroy them, the more their numbers increased.

With less than a month left until the decree of banishment was to take effect, Rabban Gamliel sought the advice of one of the Roman senators. This senator was very favorably disposed towards the Jews, and might possibly have been a secret convert himself. The senator assured

Rabban Gamliel that the law would not come to pass. The Senate had a rule that should any senator die between the time a law was passed and before it came into effect, that law was abolished. Five days before the decree was to become law, after consultation with his wife, the Jewish senator drank poison and died. The law was abolished. Just before his death, the secret Jew circumcised himself. (*Midrash Rabah, Devarim* 2:24)

NERVA RULES AFTER DOMITIAN IS ASSASSINATED 85-98 C.E.

Domitian had craved absolute power from the days of his youth. Now that he was the emperor of the mighty Roman Empire, he resented anyone else who had power. Rabban Gamliel and his *Sanhedrin* conducted their religious affairs brazenly in public as though they were an autonomous body. Many Romans were converting to Judaism. The threat of the *Sanhedrin* had to be eliminated.

Rabban Gamliel, fearing reprisals from Rome, moved the sacred assembly to Usha in the north. In this sparsely populated area, he felt more secure from prying Roman eyes.

Meanwhile, in Rome, a great sensation was stirred. A close relative of Domitian, Flavius Clemens, was considering conversion to Judaism. Clemens was a senator and former second consul of Rome. Clemens' son had personally been chosen by Domitian to be the next emperor. The thought of the son of a Jew becoming emperor stirred messianic hopes in the hearts of the remnant Jews. But pagan Romans and jealous Christians alike shuddered at the thought. When word of Clemens' religious disposition reached Domitian, the emperor had his kinsman executed.

Life for Domitian's fellow Romans was insecure, to say the least. Neither friend nor foe felt safe. With the participation of Domitian's wife, Domitian was assassinated in 96 c.e. The Senate chose Marcus Nerva as the new Caesar.

Nerva's reign lasted only sixteen months, but offered a respite from the bloodshed and treachery of the Domitian years. Nerva granted a pardon to those who had been banished by the former emperor, and he restored all property that Domitian had seized. Jews were free to worship as they saw fit, and pagans were permitted to convert openly to Judaism. The Jew Tax, although not officially abolished, was not collected with any zeal. Jews who were suspected of avoiding the tax were not persecuted. Nerva had coins issued with his profile on one side and a Judean palm leaf on the other. The inscription read, *"Fisci Judaici calmunia sublata.* Suspicions of the Jew's tax are annulled."

Nerva

The Christians, who had also been persecuted by the Roman emperors, took advantage of the new liberal government. They became arrogant and spread false rumors against the Jews. These suspicious reports were then duly

---

surrounding the Danube. He then sought to annex the land between the Euphrates and the Ganges, as Alexander had done before him. The only resistance Trajan encountered was from the Jews in these Asiatic provinces, who occupied whole towns in the lands beyond the Euphrates and enjoyed a certain amount of autonomy. They had their own religious and political leaders who stood steadfast as a block in the path of the conquering Trajan. However, by the fifteenth year of his rule, most of Mesopotamia and her Jews were under Roman dominion.

Trajan's wife gave birth to a child during the night of the Ninth of *Av* while the Jews sat in mourning. A few months later, the child died. It was the first night of *Chanukah*. The Jews asked the Elders if they should celebrate the festival or not. It was decided they should celebrate.

"When you gave birth, the Jews mourned," some Christians told the emperor's wife. "When the child died, they celebrated."

She sent a letter to her husband saying, "Instead of fighting the barbarians, come and fight against the Jews, for they have rebelled against you." (*Eichah Rabah* 1:45)

The Jews, hearing that Trajan was coming to seek revenge, rose up to protect themselves. The Jews of Mesopotamia and Judea were the first to revolt. The Judeans drove out the Roman officials, and the soldiers' garrisons were destroyed. News of the rebellion gave courage to the African Jews in Egypt, Libya and Cyprus to rise up and shake off the bonds of Rome. The Second Revolt against Rome had begun.

The African insurrection began in Cyrenaica, Liby

conveyed to the Roman officials. Rabban Gamliel and the *Sanhedrin* instituted a nineteenth blessing to the Eighteen Blessings, called *Ve'lamalshinim*. The blessing sought divine retribution against these evil talebearers.

During the tranquil era of the emperor Nerva, the seat of the *Sanhedrin* was moved back to Yavneh, and Rabban Gamliel established a great *yeshivah* in Lud.

Emperor Nerva died, and the tranquility and calm departed with him. His adopted son, Trajan the Warrior, became emperor.

CHAPTER VII
THE SECOND REVOLT

TRAJAN SEEKS REVENGE
99 C.E.

Trajan was born in the Roman colony of Italica, Spain. He was an illustrious general, the son of a distinguished warrior. The emperor Nerva, who was docile by nature, adopted Trajan to build up his own esteem in the eyes of his countrymen. Trajan had the blood of war rushing through his veins and the vision of an expanded Roman Empire filling his mind. Tranquility marked the rule of Nerva; uprising and revolt marked the reign of Trajan.

Trajan envisioned himself to be the Alexander of Rome. He first subdued the European provinces

Trajan

Exaggerated Gentile reports claimed the Jews massacred two hundred and twenty thousand Romans. From Libya, the revolt spread to Egypt. In the Egyptian capital of Alexandria, the fighting was especially fierce. The Alexandrian Jews, with the help of their Libyan brothers, were victorious.

From Egypt, the revolt spread to Cyprus in the Mediterranean Sea. Cyprus had a large Jewish population, and the Jews easily defeated their pagan oppressors. Inflated reports placed the Roman casualties at one half million Romans.

The Jews had visions of rebuilding Judea and the Holy Temple. The "exile without end" would have lasted only forty-five years. But the Sages had warned that the exile could not end by force or might; any cause for celebration was premature. (*Midrash Shir Hashirim* 2:4)

Trajan was determined to turn the Jews' vision of deliverance and dreams of Messiah into a nightmare. He entrusted two of his ablest and most bloodthirsty generals, Martius Turbo and Lucius Quietus, with the task of subduing the Jewish revolt. Turbo was placed in charge of the African campaign, and Quietus took charge of the Judean and Mesopotamian fronts. The *Sanhedrin*, anticipating the revenge of Rome, moved to Lud. Many of the Sages went into hiding with their students, for they realized that the "exile without an end" had not even begun.

Slowly and inexorably, Turbo put down the revolt. In Egypt, tens of thousands of Jews were slaughtered. The Great Synagogue of Alexandria was destroyed. In Cyprus, no Jew remained alive.

Quietus was likewise successful in ending the rebellion in Judea and Mesopotamia. He conducted a war of annihilation against the Jews. The bodies of the slain Jewish men blocked the streets and byways of the Middle Eastern cities and towns. The Jewish women, in order to avoid defilement, refused to be spared. "Do to us as you have done to our husbands and fathers," the Jewish wives and daughters said. And so, the blood of the women mingled with the blood of the men. (*Eichah Rabah* 1:45) Quietus was rewarded with governorship of Judea.

The brothers Lulianus and Pappus, the two leaders of the Jewish revolt, were captured. They were brought before Trajan to be publicly executed.

"You are descendants of Chananiah, Mishael and Azariah," the Emperor mocked them. "I am a descendant of Nebuchadnezzar. Just as your Lord wrought a miracle in those days and saved them from death, so too, let Him bring a miracle and save you."

"Our ancestors were holy men; your royal ancestor was a worthy opponent," the brothers answered. "It was fitting for a miracle to be wrought through them. But we are sinners, and you are a sinner. Neither of us is worthy of a miracle."

Before Trajan could give the order to execute the two Jewish brothers, two mutinous deputies stepped out of the crowd and attacked Trajan with clubs, mortally wounding him. (*Koheles Rabah* 3:16)

The Jewish people proclaimed that day, the twelfth of *Adar*, as a holiday. It was called Trajan Day. (*Taanis* 18b)

Trajan's dream of a conquest to the Ganges was never

realized. As the emperor lay on his deathbed, he expressed his wish that Quietus be given the title of Emperor. However, Trajan's wife Plotina informed Rome that Trajan wished his nephew Aeilus Hadrian to be his heir.

Years earlier, the Jews had moaned, "If Vespasian was a bear, then Trajan was a lion." (*Eichah Rabah* 3:10) What would they call Hadrian, the greatest butcher of them all?

HADRIAN APPEASES THE JEWS
117 C.E.

Hadrian, like his uncle Trajan, was born in Spain. Hadrian had commanded Trajan's troops in Syria during the Mesopotamian campaign. Hadrian witnessed how his uncle tried to extinguish the spirit of the Jews by slaughter and persecution. Now that the reigns of power were turned over to him, Hadrian was unsure of how the Jews would react. He feared the Jews would renew their determination to rebel and shake off the yoke of Rome. Hadrian decided that a different tactic was needed.

At first, Hadrian sought to rebuild the Holy City. The new Judean capital would be a gift of appeasement from Rome to her Jews. Throughout the empire, the Jews were to be considered and treated as any other citizen. Lulianus and

Hadrian

Pappus, the two brothers who had instigated the revolt against Trajan, were appointed as public officials to oversee the needs of the Jews. Onkelos the convert was placed in charge of the rebuilding of Jerusalem. Funds were raised throughout the Middle East to help ease the burdens created by the previous years of persecution and devastation.

The Jews began to wonder if their new-found peace was a heavenly sign that the Messianic era was approaching. Almost confirming their hopes, a decree came from Rome granting the Jews permission to rebuild their Temple. The Jews celebrated.

Even Hadrian celebrated the budding mutual respect between Judea and Rome. He had coins minted showing the Roman emperor and the "widow Jerusalem" standing near an altar on which both were preparing to offer a sacrifice.

Hadrian had engaged in many philosophical and metaphysical debates with Rabbi Yehoshua ben Chananiah. (*Bereishis Rabah* 10:3, 28:3; *Eichah Rabah* 3:9) Hadrian once exclaimed to the rabbi that he, the emperor, was greater than Moses, for the emperor was alive and Moses was dead. The sage asked Hadrian to decree in Rome that fires not be lit for three days. When the decree was declared, the emperor and the sage went atop the roof of Hadrian's palace after dark. When they looked out, they saw fires. Rabbi Yehoshua said to Hadrian, "You see, your decrees are not kept while you are still alive, whereas the decrees of Moses our teacher, who decreed that fires not be lit on the Sabbath, are still kept." (*Midrash Ruth* 3:2)

As part of the new policy of reconciliation, Hadrian claimed that the presence of the Roman soldiers in Judea was only to maintain the peace. The Jewish blacksmiths and metal workers were given the task of making the weapons for these foreign legionnaires. The suspicious Jews, fearing that one day these weapons would be turned against them, purposely made them weak. The weapons would make a grand display, but would be almost useless in battle.

Meanwhile, the favor bestowed upon the Jews stirred the jealousy and anger of the Christians living in the Holy Land. They feared that if the Temple were rebuilt and the *Sanhedrin* were given authority over the land, they would be threatened. A Christian delegation informed Rome that a Temple in Jerusalem would only encourage the Jews to rebel. (*Bereishis Rabah* 64:10)

However, Hadrian was reluctant to rescind the permission to build the Temple. Instead, he decreed that it be built elsewhere, or at least alter its original dimensions. The Jews, realizing that the Temple could not be built anywhere other than on Mount Moriah, following the dimensions stipulated by the prophets of old, understood that Hadrian had, in effect, withdrawn permission for the Temple to be built. (*ibid.*)

Many Jews from the diaspora had already gathered in the land of their forefathers and dedicated their efforts to prepare for the Temple's reconstruction. When the news reached them that they were to cease all labors, they were prepared to revolt. The Sages sent Rabbi Yehoshua ben Chananiah to calm the people. (*ibid.*)

The rabbi told a parable. A lion had a bone caught in his

throat. The stork came and, with his long beak, removed the bone. The stork asked for his reward. The lion replied, "You may go and tell everyone that you had your head in the lion's mouth and came out in peace. That is your reward." We Jews are like that stork; we too can say that we are still at peace. That is reward enough. (*ibid.*)

Rabbi Yehoshua's words managed to calm the spirit of revolt. Indeed, Rabbi Yehoshua was often able to use the power of words and insight where others thought force and might were required. It is no wonder that when Rabbi Yehoshua died the Sages said, "Advice and thought are gone forever." (*Sotah* 49b)

About this time, the daughter of Hadrian was found murdered, and the Jews were accused of the crime. Hadrian was furious. If the culprits were not found, all the Jews would suffer. The brothers Lulianus and Pappus "confessed" to the crime in order to save their brethren. Hadrian had them executed in the city of Lud. (*Rashi Taanis* 18b)

Our Sages have said concerning these two righteous brothers, "No creature may even stand in their portion of the World to Come." (*Rashi Taanis* 18b; *Bava Basra* 10b)

THE GREAT PERSECUTION

The conciliatory policies of Hadrian came to an abrupt halt. Three factors brought about this change. First, Hadrian's desire for revenge for the murder of his daughter was in no way satisfied by the execution of the two brothers, who confessed falsely out of the righteous desire to protect their countrymen. Second, the Christians and Samarians constantly agitated against the Jews. But perhaps the strongest element that brought about the change was that the other conquered provinces adopted the Roman lifestyle and culture, whereas the Jews stubbornly held onto their traditional ways and beliefs. Hadrian's patience was at an end, and he was now prepared to wage a religious and cultural war against the Jews. The battle had begun centuries ago when the Angel of Esau had fought with Jacob. Hadrian, the descendant of Esau, would now complete the struggle against the descendants of Jacob. (*Bereishis Rabah* 77:3)

Hadrian decreed many laws against the Jews. These decrees had a twofold purpose. In order to limit the Jewish population of Judea, it was forbidden for any diaspora Jew to emigrate to the Holy Land. In order to put an end to the religious and cultural identity of the Jews, it was decreed that the Jews were forbidden to observe the rites of circumcision, the laws of the Sabbath and family purity. (*Meilah* 17a) A violation of any decree was punishable by death. Any Gentile seeking conversion was also subject to the same penalty.

A Jew, Imikantron, sent a letter to Hadrian. "If you oppose circumcision because it is barbaric," he wrote, "then persecute the Ishmaelites, for they, too, circumcise their males. If you despise the Sabbath because it makes people lazy, then also persecute the Samarians, for they, too, rest on the Sabbath. If you simply hate the Jews, their Lord will exact punishment from you." (*Koheles Rabah* 2:15)

Hadrian sought the writer of the offensive letter. When Imikantron was found, the emperor asked why he had consciously invited the imperial wrath. The Jew answered that he realized the emperor would execute him for his offense, but execution would relieve him of three anxieties—his pangs of hunger, his wife's pangs and his children's pangs. Hadrian had made the desire for death sweeter than the lust for life. The emperor had the Jew beheaded. (*ibid.*)

Rabbi Reuven ben Istrobli shaved the upper portion of his head to disguise himself as a Roman. He approached the Roman senators and said, "If a man has an enemy, does the enemy wish the man to be rich or poor?"

"Poor," the senators answered.

"Then prohibit the Jews from working on their Sabbath," Rabbi Reuven continued. "If a man has an enemy, does the enemy wish the man to be strong or weak?"

"Weak," they answered.

"Then order them to circumcise their males," Rabbi Reuven said. "If a man has an enemy, does the enemy wish the man's numbers to increase or decrease?"

"Decrease," the senators answered.

"Then force the Jews to keep their laws of family purity."

The senators agreed with the disguised rabbi's arguments and repealed the decrees. (*Meilah* 17a)

When it was discovered that Rabbi Reuven was a Jew, they realized they had been fooled and quickly reinstated the decrees. (*ibid.*)

The rabbis saw that the very lives of the Jews were in danger because they refused to forsake the Torah. Rabbi Yishmael taught that it should be decreed that, for the time being, no more Jewish marriages take place. In that way, family purity would not have to be kept and no male children would have to be circumcised. But Rabbi Yishmael knew that the people would not keep this ruling and, therefore, said, "Let them transgress unwittingly rather than violate the ruling willingly." (*Bava Basra* 60b)

To further insult the Jews and make them the objects of scorn, no Jew was permitted to enter Jerusalem, and the head of a swine was placed over the southern gate of the city.

None of these decrees deterred the Jews from adhering to the ways of their ancestors. Rabban Shimon, the son of Gamliel II, publicly circumcised his son. (*Avodah Zarah* 10b) Roman spies began walking the streets to ensure that the decrees were being followed. The Jews invented signals to let the people know a circumcision was to take place that day so they could attend. In the town of Bornai, the sound of millstones grinding signaled the occasion. In the village of Baror Chail, lit oil lamps were the sign. (*Sanhedrin* 32b)

The sellers of foodstuffs in Judea had to sell non-kosher foods together with kosher food to escape detection. One innkeeper would see if the lodgers would wash their hands or not to determine whether they were Romans or Jews dressed in Roman clothing. (*Bamidbar Rabah* 20:21) One Jew did not wash and, as a result was served swine. (*Bereishis Rabah* 82:8)

Aquilas, the nephew of Hadrian, sought to convert and become a Jew. (*Shir Hashirim Rabah* 1:11) Hadrian could not fathom such a desire. "See how I have degraded and slain them?" he said to his nephew. "Why do you wish to join their ranks and endure their sufferings?"

Aquilas replied that even the lowest among the Jews knows that the Lord created the universe, what was created on each day and how long ago the world was created. The Jews possess the law of truth, and upon it the world stands.

Hadrian recommended that Aquilas study the Torah but not convert or have himself circumcised.

Aquilas answered that even the wisest in the kingdom cannot study Torah unless he is circumcised. And so, Aquilas left his uncle and became a Jew. (*Shemos Rabah* 30:12)

Hadrian demanded that the Jews look like Romans. He required all Jews to shave their heads and beards. (*Eichah Rabah* 5:1) All signs of circumcision were forcibly removed. (*Rashi Yevamos* 72a)

A Jew once passed before the emperor Hadrian. The Jew greeted the emperor. The emperor had him executed.

"How dare a lowly Jew greet the mighty emperor!" he exclaimed.

Another Jew passed by, and seeing what had happened to his friend, did not greet the emperor. Hadrian had him executed.

"How dare a lowly Jew not greet the mighty emperor!" he exclaimed.

A senator, witnessing what transpired, asked Hadrian, "Both of them are executed?"

Angrily Hadrian responded, "Don't you tell me how to kill these Jews." (*Eichah Rabah* 3:9)

When asked why the Jews suffer so much at the hands of their enemies, Rabbi Nosson replied, "It makes us more

beloved to our Creator. Though we are persecuted, we remain in the Holy Land and do the *mitzvos*. When a man asks his fellow, 'Why are you being taken to be beheaded?' he replies, 'I have circumcised my son.' 'Why are you being taken to be burned at the stake?' 'I studied the Torah.' 'Why are you being taken to be crucified?' 'I ate *matzah* on Passover.' 'Why are you being taken to be tortured?' 'I took the four species on *Sukkos*.'" (*Mechiltah* 20,6)

With one more decree, Hadrian pushed the Jews beyond the point of tolerance. Hadrian decreed that a pagan temple be built on the Temple Mount. The conditions for a renewed Judean uprising were now present. All that was lacking was a military leader to spearhead the revolt, and such a savior came upon the scene.

CHAPTER VIII
THE THIRD REVOLT

THE STAR OF JACOB
125 C.E.

Nothing is known of the family and early life of the charismatic Shimon bar Kosiba. The great sage and spiritual leader of the Jewish people, Rabbi Akiva, upon witnessing the almost supernatural military skills of Bar Kosiba, proclaimed Shimon to be the divinely appointed savior of the Jews—the Messiah. (*Eichah Rabah* 2:4)

Rabbi Akiva had taught that, based on the prophecy of Haggai, the "*galus* without end" would be short-lived. A king from Judah would arise, and he would deliver the Jews. Rabbi Akiva believed Bar Kosiba to be that King of Judah. (*Sanhedrin* 97b)

Rabbi Akiva called Bar Kosiba, Bar Kokhba, the son of the star, referring to the Biblical verse "a star has arisen in Jacob." (Numbers 24:17) The majority of the Sages agreed with Rabbi Akiva. They, too, recognized Bar Kokhba as the Messiah. (*Rambam Hilchos Melachim* 11:3) A few, more skeptical Sages called him Bar Koziba, the son of deceit, for they were not convinced that the time of Messiah had come.

Rabbi Yochanan ben Torta declared, "Akiva, grass will grow on your chin, before the Messiah comes." (*Yerushalmi Taanis* 4:5)

Metal weight with the name Bar Kosiba and the rosette design

Jews flocked from all corners of the Roman Empire to the banner of Bar Kokhba. Four hundred thousand inspired Jews answered the call. (*Yerushalmi Taanis* 4:5) They left their homes and possessions to learn the ways of war. Two hundred thousand were put to the test of courage by biting off the end of their finger. (*Korban Haeidah, ibid.*) The Sages objected to the self-mutilation and suggested a test of uprooting a sapling while riding at full gallop. Another two hundred thousand passed this test. (*Yerushalmi Taanis* 4:5)

In the days of old, the prophet Jeremiah had warned the Jewish people against four things: Do not rebel against the government, do not try to hasten the end of days, do not reveal the mysteries of Torah, and do not leave the diaspora by force. If so, for what purpose will the Messiah come? Bar

Kokhba did not heed the warning and tried to hasten the end of days by force, proclaiming himself to be the Messiah. (*Eichah Rabah* 2:7)

The Roman governor of Judea, Tinius Rufus, called by the Jews Tyrannus Rufus, Rufus the Terrible, was powerless against the forces of Bar Kokhba. Hadrian sent two generals to come to the aid of Tinius Rufus, Publius Marcellus and Lolius Urbicius. They brought legions from Phoenicia, Arabia and Egypt, but even these ablest of military men could not subdue the messianic fervor. Within a year's time, Bar Kokhba recaptured nine hundred and eighty-five villages and constructed fifty fortresses.

There were Jews who had earlier converted to paganism when the hand of Rome lay heavily upon the Jews. They underwent a surgical procedure to remove the sign of circumcision. That was their only way to escape the penalties of the Jew Tax. Now that the Messiah had come, they underwent another circumcision and re-entered the divine covenant. Other Jews had their sign of circumcision removed by the Romans by force. They, too, performed a second circumcision. (*Rashi Yevamos* 72a)

Bar Kokhba had Roman coins restruck, proclaiming "Freedom of Jerusalem" and "Freedom of Israel."

The captured Romans were treated with dignity and honor. However, the Christians of Jewish lineage were branded as traitors and informers and were brought to trial. Though the rule of the *Sanhedrin* was now the law of the land and the death penalty could have been exacted, mercy was shown, and the guilty departed the courts with only a harsh reprimand.

Hadrian, who had expected a quick victory, was becoming the object of mockery. In Britain, he was also faced with revolt, but the Roman general, Julius Severus, dashed Britain's hope for freedom. Hadrian called Severus to the Judean front. Judea had to be recaptured and subdued at all costs.

Upon Severus' arrival in Judea, he saw that there was no one battlefront. The entire land had to be recaptured piece by piece. Therefore, he resolved not to expect a quick victory. His troops went from city to city, from town to town, besieging the cities and murdering the inhabitants.

Severus promised amnesty to all those Jews who surrendered. Many Jews, seeing the successes of the Romans, feared that the Messiah had, indeed, not yet arrived, and so they surrendered. Many Jews were taken to the Valley of Rimmon.

"Before I finish eating my cake and leg of fowl, see to it that not one Jew remains alive," Severus ordered.

The soldiers complied, and a terrible massacre took place in the valley. (*Eichah Rabah* 1:16)

Tunnels in underground cities constructed by the Jews during the Bar Kokhba uprising

The tides of war were quickly turning against Bar Kokhba. He blamed the Lord for his losses and declared, "Lord, if You do not march with us, then at least do not march against us." (*Yerushalmi Taanis* 4:5) The great Sages, who had endorsed Bar Kokhba as the illustrious savior, began to have their doubts.

RABBI AKIVA'S RISE TO GREATNESS

The intense messianic zeal implanted at this time was attributed to the greatest of the Sages, Rabbi Akiva ben Yosef. Many of our Sages were born into illustrious families and were predestined, as it were, to greatness. This was not the case with Rabbi Akiva. He was the son of a convert father, a descendant of the enemy general Sisera. (*Seder Hadoros*) In his younger years, he was not only an ignorant shepherd, but he also resented scholars. (*Pesachim* 49b)

Rabbi Akiva was a humble shepherd for the wealthy Kalba Savua. (*Gittin* 56a) Kalba Savua's daughter saw many admirable qualities in the ignorant shepherd and married him against the wishes of her father. (*Kesubos* 62b) When Kalba Savua heard of the marriage, he vowed to disown the newlywed couple. The poor couple had to endure their poverty by sleeping on mats of straw, for they did not even own a bed. In the mornings, Akiva had to pick the straw out of his wife's hair.

"Oh, that I could afford a gold hair-pin with the city of Jerusalem engraved upon it," bemoaned Akiva.

The prophet Elijah once appeared before them and

cried out, "Give me straw! My wife is about to give birth, and she has no straw to lie upon."

Akiva and his wife took comfort that there was someone less fortunate than they. (*Nedarim* 50a)

Once while tending a flock, Akiva noticed some dripping water wearing away a stone. "If water can make an impression on cold hard stone, surely the words of Torah, which are compared to water, can make an impression on my mind, which is also like a hard stone." (*Avos d'Rabbi Nassan* 6) Akiva's wife advised him to leave home and study Torah. He went to Lud and attended the House of Study of Rabbi Eliezer and Rabbi Yehoshua for twelve years. (*Nedarim* 50a)

Upon his return home, he overheard a cynical elderly man remark to Akiva's wife that Akiva had abandoned her. His wife replied that she wished he would abandon her for another twelve years, so he would be able to continue his studies and teaching. Seeing that his wife had granted him permission to return to his studies, Akiva resumed his learning. After the second twelve years had passed, Rabbi Akiva returned home with twenty-four thousand disciples. (*Nedarim* 60a)

Rabbi Akiva's wife tried to make her way through the crowd of disciples to see her husband. One of the disciples, not knowing who the poverty-stricken woman was, attempted to block her, but Rabbi Akiva commanded, "Let her pass, for my learning and your learning is because of her."

When Kalba Savua heard what had become of his once despised son-in-law, he asked that his vow to deprive his daughter and her saintly husband be annulled. (*Nedarim* 60a)

Rabbi Akiva became wealthy without abandoning his teaching or studies. In addition to the support of his father-in-law, he once found washed ashore the decorative head of a ram that had graced the prow of a ship. Inside were many golden dinars. Another time, some sailors presented him with a hollow log. It, too, contained treasure. (*ibid.*)

Rabbi Akiva once borrowed a great sum of money for the House of Learning from a woman. He pledged the Lord and the sea as guarantors for the loan. When the loan was almost due, Rabbi Akiva took ill. The woman saw that she was not about to be repaid. She went to the edge of the sea and called to the Lord, asking for her money. At that same moment, the emperor's daughter was overcome with a fit of insanity. She threw a coin-laden chest into the sea. That chest floated to where the woman was standing. When Rabbi Akiva recovered from his illness, he approached the woman with apologies and repaid the debt. The woman explained that the Lord had already repaid the money, and even gave her back more than she loaned. She told Rabbi Akiva to keep his money, and she also gave him the excess that was in the chest. (*Ran, Nedarim* 60a) One of the few indulgences of Rabbi Akiva was to give his wife a piece of gold jewelry with an engraving of Jerusalem. (*Shabbos* 59b)

Rabbi Akiva was truly blessed, blessed with an inspiring wife, blessed with wisdom and blessed with wealth. The greatest school of learning in Judea was in the city of Bnei Brak. It was headed by Rabban Gamliel II. Once, when a great controversy broke out in the school, there was talk of replacing Rabban Gamliel with Rabbi Akiva. Had it not been for Rabbi Akiva's humble lineage, he would have been given the position.

Rabbi Akiva was about fifty-seven years of age and already an accomplished teacher at the time the Temple was destroyed. A few years after the destruction, many of the students of Rabbi Akiva were felled by a plague. The Sages attributed the cause of this divine retribution to the young scholars who did not accord each other proper respect. Twenty-four thousand pairs of students died. The Torah world was devastated. Rabbi Akiva went to the south and taught Torah to Rabbi Meir, Rabbi Yehudah, Rabbi Yossi, Rabbi Shimon and Rabbi Elazar ben Shamuah, and together they re-established the oral tradition of Torah. (*Yevamos* 62b)

During the time of the great persecution, the Romans had guards stationed outside the House of Learning of Rabbi Akiva. When it was time to recite the *Shema*, they had to say the words in such a low tone that they could not hear their own words. (*Tosefta Berachos* 2)

During the early years of the Bar Kokhba rebellion, Rabbi Akiva believed that divine deliverance was certain to come. He was Bar Kokhba's greatest supporter and proclaimed him to be the Messiah. Alas, the dream of redemption was not to be. During the campaigns of Julius Severus, Rabbi Akiva was captured and imprisoned.

In an earlier time, Pappus ben Yehudah found Rabbi Akiva assembling students and publicly teaching them Torah. Pappus asked, "Akiva, aren't you afraid of the government?"

Rabbi Akiva replied with a parable. A fox walking alongside a river saw a school of fish swimming to and fro. The fox asked from whom were they fleeing. The fish replied that they were fleeing from the men who cast nets. The fox wondered why the fish did not come onto dry land where they would live together with the fox in peace. The fish said to the fox, "Are you the one they call clever? You are not so clever after all, but rather foolish. If we live in fear in the water which gives us life, how much more so on the land which means certain death."

Rabbi Akiva explained that the Jewish people are like those fish. If we live in fear while studying Torah which gives us life, how much more would we have to fear if we lived without the Torah. (*Berachos* 61b)

On the fifth day of *Tishrei*, Rabbi Akiva was arrested and thrown into prison in Caesaria. (*Megilas Taanis* and *Semachos* 8) Pappus was also arrested and put in the cell next to Rabbi Akiva. Rabbi Akiva wondered why Pappus had been arrested.

"Fortunate are you, Rabbi Akiva," Pappus told the sage, "for you were seized for teaching Torah, while I, Pappus, was seized for idle things." (*Berachos* 61b)

Rabbi Akiva continued to give *halachic* rulings while imprisoned. (*Gittin* 66a) He adhered to all the precepts of the Torah and even risked his life to fulfill the rabbinical requirement of washing before partaking of food. (*Eruvin* 21b)

The Romans decreed that anyone bestowing rabbinical ordination would be punished by death. Whomever received ordination would likewise be killed, and the city in which the ordination took place would be razed to the ground as far out as the Sabbath boundary (two thousand cubits). Rabbi Yehudah ben Bava went to the mountains between Usha and Shefaram, outside their Sabbath boundaries, and ordained Rabbi Meir, Rabbi Yehudah, Rabbi Shimon, Rabbi Yossi, and Rabbi Elazar ben Shamuah.

When word of the ordination reached the Romans, Rabbi Yehudah ben Bava told his students to flee. The newly ordained rabbis asked what would become of their teacher, Rabbi Yehudah ben Bava. Rabbi Yehudah convinced them that the Romans would regard him as a worthless stone. The students fled. When the soldiers discovered Rabbi Yehudah ben Bava, they pierced his body with three hundred iron spears. (*Sanhedrin* 13b)

Five days after Rabbi Akiva was imprisoned, he was taken out to be executed. That was on the eve of *Yom Kippur*. (*Slichas El Elokim Etzakah*) As they were taking him out, it was time to recite the *Shema*. While the Romans were scraping his flesh with iron combs, the holy sage was accepting the yoke of Heaven. His students who were brought to witness the painful torture of their teacher cried out, "So far?"

Rabbi Akiva replied, "All my life I sought to fulfill the verse 'And you shall love G-d your Lord with all your soul.' Now that I have the chance, shall I not seize it?" He prolonged the word "*Echad*" (One), so that he expired while proclaiming the Unity of the Creator. (*Berachos* 61b)

One of the outstanding students of Rabbi Akiva was Rabbi Shimon bar Yochai, usually referred to simply as Rabbi Shimon. He studied under Rabbi Akiva in Bnei Brak for thirteen years. (*Vayikrah Rabah* 21:7) While Rabbi Akiva was imprisoned, Rabbi Shimon begged his teacher to continue their studies together. Rabbi Akiva refused, because it would place the student's life in danger. Rabbi Shimon persisted, but Rabbi Akiva was adamant.

"More than the calf wishes to nurse from its mother, the mother wishes to nurse her calf," Rabbi Akiva told his student.

"But the life of the calf is the one that is endangered if it does not nurse," replied Rabbi Shimon. "I am that calf." (*Pesachim* 112a)

Rabbi Shimon was sitting with Rabbi Yehudah bar Elai and Rabbi Yossi. Rabbi Yehudah expressed how great were the markets, bridges and bathhouses the Romans had built. Rabbi Yossi did not comment. Rabbi Shimon said that the Romans build markets to house the places of ill repute, bridges to collect tolls and bathhouses for their own pleasures. Another man, Yehudah, the son of righteous converts, overheard their conversation and innocently retold it at home. A government informer overheard Yehudah's comments and reported it to the government.

An official came and told Rabbi Yehudah, "Since you praised us, your position shall be elevated. Rabbi Yossi, who was silent, shall be exiled to Sephoris. Shimon, who mocked us, shall be executed."

Rabbi Shimon and his son Rabbi Elazar hid in the house of learning. As the officials became more and more frustrated in their attempts to capture him, Rabbi Shimon feared they would torture his wife to reveal their hiding place. Rabbi Shimon and his son left the house of learning and went into the wilderness. They found a cave and remained hidden inside for thirteen years. (*Shabbos* 33b)

Rabbi Akiva and Rabbi Yehudah ben Bava were dead. Rabbi Shimon and Rabbi Elazar were in hiding. The spiritual leadership was gone from the rebellion, victims of Julius Severus' march of doom. It took Severus several years and more than fifty battles to recapture Judea. When Jerusalem was retaken by the Romans, the governor Tinius Rufus brought a plow to the Temple Mount and plowed it up. That occurred on the ninth day of *Av*. (*Rambam, Taanis* 5:3) In the end, all the cities and strongholds were recaptured except one, Betar. Betar became the last haven for the Jews, and it was here in Betar that Bar Kokhba, the Star of Jacob, would fall. (*Yerushalmi Taanis* 4:5)

THE LAST REFUGE
132 C.E.

The great city of Betar was the last refuge of the Jews. It was southwest of Jerusalem, not far from the Mediterranean Sea. It was surrounded on three sides by deep valleys, providing a natural barrier against invasion. It had its own wellsprings within the city; an invader would be unable to cut off their water supply. A strong wall surrounded the city, making it almost impregnable.

Betar was a center for Torah studies with hundreds of houses of learning, each with hundreds of students. It was a city at peace with itself.

The people of Betar were confident that Bar Kokhba

would miraculously deliver them from the Roman threat. Schoolchildren would mock the Romans, "Should they come against us, we will stab them with our pens." (*Eichah Rabah* 3:9)

When the Temple had still been standing in Jerusalem, there had been great envy and animosity between the aristocrats of the Holy City and the natives of Betar. When the people of Betar would come to Jerusalem for the festivals, they would become the objects of mockery and scorn. The people of Betar prayed that their feet should fail them so they would be unable to return in the future. They hoped the roads leading to the city would become impassable, so that no one would be able to make the pilgrimage. When the Temple was destroyed and the Holy City devastated, Betar was smug. (*Eichah Rabah* 2:4) But "he that rejoices at calamity shall not go unpunished." (*Mishlei* 8:5)

During the three-year siege of Betar, Rabbi Elazar of Modim, the uncle of Bar Kokhba, fasted and prayed, "Lord of the Universe, sit not in judgment today."

Hadrian was weary from waiting for the city to surrender, and was preparing to withdraw his troops. Rabbi Elazar's prayers were almost answered when a traitorous old Jew told Hadrian to wait a bit more.

"As long as that pious rooster crows, you will not be able to overtake the city," he told the emperor. "But wait, do not withdraw. I shall enable you to conquer the city this very day." (*Eichah Rabah* 2:4 and *Yerushalmi Taanis* 4:5)

The traitor entered the city and found Rabbi Elazar engaged in prayer. He pretended to whisper something into the Sage's ear. People saw the traitor conversing with

Rabbi Elazar and reported it to Bar Kokhba. Bar Kokhba had the traitor brought before him and demanded to know what had transpired between him and Rabbi Elazar.

"If I tell you, the Emperor Hadrian will kill me," the traitor said. "If I do not tell you, you will kill me. Better I die at your hands. Elazar said that he wants to surrender Betar to the Romans." (*ibid.*)

Bar Kokhba had his uncle Rabbi Elazar brought before him. The uncle claimed he knew of no conversation with anyone, for he was engrossed in his prayers. The disbelieving Bar Kokhba flew into a rage, kicked the holy sage and killed him. That day, the very life and breath of Betar was extinguished. (*ibid.*)

The rabbis had an oral tradition that the Messiah could smell truth. They decided to test this "Messiah." A case was brought before him to judge. The "Messiah" ruled incorrectly. He could not smell the truth. And so, the Sages killed the so-called Messiah. (*Sanhedrin* 93b)

Betar was conquered, and the head of Bar Kokhba was brought to Hadrian.

"Who killed him?" inquired the emperor.

The traitor claimed that he had killed Bar Kokhba. Hadrian asked to see the rest of the body. When the betrayer went to retrieve the corpse, he found a snake coiled about it. He reported this to Hadrian who exclaimed, "It was the Lord Who killed him." (*Eichah Rabah* 2:4 and *Yerushalmi Taanis* 4:5)

The slaughter that took place in Betar was unimaginable. Men, women and children were murdered with equal abandon. In sheer numbers, the victims surpassed the fallen during Titus' conquest of Jerusalem, even more than the butcher Nevuzaradan had killed during the destruction of the First Temple. The tragedy of Betar equaled the destruction of the Temple itself. (*Rambam Taanis* 5:3) Like the destruction of the First and Second Temples, the destruction of Betar occurred on the ninth day of *Av*. (*Mishnah Taanis* 4:6)

The blood flowed in Betar like raging torrents of water. Horses nearly drowned in the red pools. Great rocks were moved by its rushing course, and the stream of blood flowed out into the sea. (*Yerushalmi Taanis* 4:5)

For seven years, the neighboring vineyards were cultivated without fertilizer. The vines yielded their fruits, nourished from the blood of the victims of Betar. (*Gittin* 57a) Hadrian owned a vineyard that was eighteen *mil* long and eighteen *mil* wide. He had a fence made around the entire vineyard out of the corpses of Betar's fallen. Hadrian decreed that the bodies never be buried. They would serve as a monument and a lesson to those who contemplated rebellion. (*Yerushalmi Taanis* 4:5)

The Lord also wanted a lesson to be learned. It was not the might of Hadrian that had conquered Betar, it was the sins of the Jews. And so, miraculously, the bodies of the slain did not decompose, but remained preserved until many years later when permission was granted that they be buried. (*Yerushalmi Taanis* 4:5)

The tens of thousands of schoolchildren who threatened to stave off the Romans with their pens were wrapped in their scrolls and burned alive. Only a single child managed to escape, Shimon ben Gamliel. (*Eichah Rabah* 3:9)

Roman battalions were set up along the main roads of Judea to capture and execute the fleeing survivors of the holocaust. Many Jews stayed off the roads and sought refuge in the mountain caves. These refugees had little or no food, and starvation began to take its course. In desperation, they fed upon the corpses of their fallen brothers. (*Eichah Rabah* :16)

One man had gone out each morning looking for a corpse to eat. That particular day he came across a body, the body of his father. He buried his father and set a marker to indicate the site. When he returned to the cave, a friend asked what he had found that day.

"Nothing," replied the first one.

The friend decided he would go out to try his luck. He found the buried corpse, brought it back and cooked the remains. The friend shared his meal with the first man who had brought back nothing to eat. While they were eating, the first man asked his friend where he had found the corpse since he had looked earlier and found nothing. The friend said that he found it buried with a marker over the gravesite.

The first man began to choke and cried out, "Woe, woe to me. I have eaten from the flesh of my father to keep alive." (*Eichah Rabah* 1:16)

Captives were dragged by the thousands and sold in the

slave markets of Gaza and Hebron. So many were offered for sale that it took only a few coins to purchase a slave. Many were taken on ships to Egypt to be sold.

Not all these captives made it to the land where their forefathers were enslaved. Many ships sank because they were overburdened with their human cargo. Many Jews succumbed to hunger and starvation.

Jerusalem was rebuilt as a Roman city and garrison. The name of the once proud and noble city was changed to Aelia Capitolina so that Jerusalem would be forgotten. Inside the northern gate, a great column was erected with a larger than life statue of the emperor Hadrian standing upon it in a defiant pose of victory. Upon the Temple Mount, a pagan temple was erected to the Roman god Jupiter Capitolina. Tinius Rufus and the Roman soldiers stood on the steps of their pagan temple and celebrated the conquest of Judea.

But although the Jewish people were conquered, they were not defeated. The next dark and long chapter of Jewish history is itself a story of extraordinary heroism. For two thousand years, the Jews have withstood persecution and emnity, repeated massacres and tragic desertions and their continual devotion to the Torah has not wavered. They have defended themselves with their spirits, their hearts and their minds, rather than with their arms, and they have been successful in sustaining the spirit of the Torah in the hostile environment of a seemingly endless diaspora. Yet even in the darkest of times, the Jewish people have kept alive the eternal hope that the arrival of *Mashiach* is imminent and that once again Jerusalem and the Holy Temple will be rebuilt, this time to last forever.

APPENDIX
FROM THE MIDRASH

THE MIDRASHIC ACCOUNT OF THE TEN MARTYRS[1]

When the Lord created the trees, they took great pride in their height and raised themselves upward. When the Lord created metal, the trees lowered themselves and cried out, "Woe is to us, for the Holy Blessed One has created something which can cut us down."

The Holy Blessed One told the tree, "If there is peace among you, who will give the wooden handle to the ax to cut you down?"

After the destruction of the Temple, the sinners among us took pride and said, "What loss is there in the destruction of the Temple? We still have among us the scholars who will teach the world the Torah and the commandments." The Lord placed it in the heart of the emperor of Rome to study the Torah of Moses from the Sages and the Elders. The iron ax of Rome now had the handle from the tree's wood, for

Torah is the Tree of Life.

The emperor commenced from the beginning of the Torah and studied until the portion of civil law. When he reached the section concerning kidnapping and selling the victim, he called for the ten wisest men in Israel and locked them inside the palace. They were brought before him and seated upon golden chairs.

"I have a difficult question to ask of you," he said. "I want you to tell me only the truth. If one kidnapped a fellow Jew and sold him, what is the law?"

The elders answered, "The Torah says the crime is punishable with death."

"If that be the case, all of you are to be put to death."

The elders objected, "But surely we have not kidnapped anyone."

"Joseph's brothers sold him into slavery," the emperor explained. "They deserved the penalty of death. If they were alive, I would have them killed, but since they are no longer here, you must carry the sin and punishment of your ancestors."

The bewildered elders requested three days to see if they could find any argument against the emperor's reasoning.[2] They agreed that if they could not exonerate themselves, they would submit to the penalty.

Rabbi Yishmael the High Priest prepared himself with sanctity, immersed himself in a pool, wrapped himself with his *tallis* and put on his *tefillin*. He uttered the Great Name and ascended to the heavens to see if the emperor's words were decreed by the Lord Himself.

The spirit carried him upward into the sixth heaven

where he met the angel Gabriel. Gabriel trembled and asked, "Are you Yishmael who glows with the radiance of an angel, whom the Lord praises each day?"

"I am."

"Why are you in the heavens?"

"I wish to know if the emperor's decree was sealed by the Holy One."

"And if it wasn't, what could you do to abolish it?"

"I would utter the Holy Name."

"Fortunate are the children of Abraham, Isaac and Jacob," Gabriel declared, "for the Holy One has revealed to them the Name which has not been revealed to us. Yishmael, my son, I have heard from behind the Divine Curtain that the heavens have decreed that ten wise men of Israel will be killed by the evil government."

Rabbi Yishmael wondered why retribution had not been carried out in an earlier generation.

Gabriel explained, "By your life, Yishmael, since Joseph was sold until today there have never been ten wise men at one time who compared to the ten brothers of Joseph."

Why did the angel Gabriel tremble when he saw Rabbi Yishmael? Why did Gabriel call Rabbi Yishmael "my son"? Before Rabbi Yishmael was born, his mother had said to his father, "We are getting old, and we have no son or daughter who will inherit from us. What can we do?"

"After the next time you immerse in the *mikveh*," her husband replied, "should you see anything displeasing, return and immerse again."

Shortly thereafter, the wife went to immerse in the *mikveh*. While walking home, she saw a dog. She returned to the *mikveh* and immersed again. She then saw a swine, and again she returned. This happened eighty times. The angel Gabriel saw what was happening. He assumed the image of her husband Elisha and stood near the entrance. He accompanied her home. That night she conceived Yishmael. The child radiated with the glow of an angel, the angel Gabriel. It was said of Rabbi Yishmael that he was one of the seven most handsome men ever created.

When Gabriel saw that Rabbi Yishmael had sadly resigned himself of his fate, the angel said, "I shall reveal to you one more secret. The angel of Rome is Samael. When he heard that the Lord sealed your fate, he rejoiced and called out, 'I am victorious over the archangel Michael.'

"The Lord called for Samael and said to him in a stern voice, 'Samael, choose one of these two: either the ten Sages should live, or Rome will be afflicted.'

"Samael replied, 'I would rather Rome be afflicted than have the Sages live.'

"The Lord called the great angel Metatron, the scribe, and told him to record and seal that Rome would suffer plague for six months, and fire and sulfur for six months. 'Let them suffer so that no one would be willing to buy all of Rome for a *perutah*.'"

The anguish of Rabbi Yishmael was appeased.

As Rabbi Yishmael was departing, he saw an Altar near the Divine Throne. Rabbi Yishmael inquired as to what kind of offering is brought upon the Heavenly Altar. Gabriel answered that the archangel Michael offers the spirits of the righteous men upon it.

Rabbi Yishmael returned to the earthly sphere and told

the elders, "Purify yourselves and put on burial shrouds. It has been decreed in heaven that ten wise men should die." They wept because of their fate. But they also rejoiced, for the Lord had compared them to the sainted ten brothers of Joseph.[3]

The elders began to occupy themselves with the laws of the third chapter of tractate *Pesachim* when the executioner came in with his sword drawn.

"Even now you occupy yourselves with Torah," he murmured.

He then brought Rabban Shimon ben Gamliel and Rabbi Yishmael before the emperor and the great men of Rome.

"Who shall be first?" the emperor asked.

Rabban Shimon ben Gamliel arose. "I am the prince, son of a prince, a descendant of King David of blessed memory. I shall be killed first."

Rabbi Yishmael stood up. "I am the High Priest, the son of the High Priest, a descendant of Aaron the Priest. I shall be killed first."

The emperor decided that lots be cast. The lots fell to Rabban Shimon ben Gamliel. The emperor called for the executioner to cut off the head of Rabban Shimon ben Gamliel. The executioner severed the holy rabbi's head.

Rabbi Yishmael picked up the head and placed it in his lap and cried with bitter tears. Rabbi Yishmael placed his eyes and mouth against the eyes and mouth of Rabban Shimon ben Gamliel. "Oh, Torah! Oh, reward! The tongue that made clear the words of Torah in seventy languages now licks the dust." And he moaned and cried bitterly over

Rabban Shimon ben Gamliel.

The emperor exclaimed, "Old man, why do you cry for your friend? Better cry for yourself!"

"I do cry for myself," Rabbi Yishmael answered. "My friend was greater in Torah and wisdom, and his reward is greater. He is already receiving his reward, while I am still here."

The emperor's daughter was looking through the window and saw the great beauty of Rabbi Yishmael the High Priest. She was overcome with pity and told her father she had a request. The emperor told his daughter that she could ask for anything but not to spare the life of that man, for the emperor had already sworn to kill him. The daughter then asked for the skin of Rabbi Yishmael's head to place by the mirror in her room.

The emperor ordered that the skin of the head of Rabbi Yishmael be removed while he was still alive. When they reached the place of his *tefillin*, Rabbi Yishmael let out a great and bitter cry. The heavens and earth trembled. He cried out again and the Heavenly Throne trembled.

"Why do you cry now and not at the beginning?" the emperor asked.

"I cry now because you have taken the *tefillin* from me," answered Rabbi Yishmael.

The ministering angels were watching from above and said to the Lord, "For this righteous man to whom you have shown the treasures of the heavens and the secrets of the world below, is it a just reward to die such a horrible death at the hands of that evil man?"

The Lord answered, "Let it be. His merits will protect

many generations to come. Let the decree stand, and no one shall try to abolish it."

That moment, a Heavenly Voice called out, "Yishmael, if you cry out once more, the heavens and earth shall revert to emptiness and void."

Rabbi Yishmael remained silent.

The emperor asked, "Do you still believe in your Lord?"

Rabbi Yishmael answered, "Even until death, I have faith in Him." With that utterance, Rabbi Yishmael died.[4]

[In] later [years], Rabbi Akiva was imprisoned. It was five days before *Yom Kippur*. Rabbi Akiva could expound upon every stroke of the Torah scribe's pen. He was able to reveal the meaning of Torah as it was given to Moses on Sinai. He had been held in prison until the emperor could return from battle to witness the execution. The emperor returned on *Yom Kippur*. He ordered that Rabbi Akiva's skin be removed with iron combs. Rabbi Akiva proclaimed the great justice and righteousness of the Creator. A Heavenly Voice called out, "Fortunate are you, Rabbi Akiva, for you were just and righteous and your soul departs in justice and righteousness."[5]

They returned the body of the aged rabbi to the prison cell. The door was left ajar; the guards had fallen asleep. Elijah, the prophet and priest, carried away the remains of Rabbi Akiva. Rabbi Yehoshua Hagarsi met Elijah and asked him, "Are you not a priest? How can you carry a corpse?"

"It is Rabbi Akiva," Elijah answered. "He was pure and holy and cannot be defiled."

Rabbi Yehoshua Hagarsi accompanied Elijah until they came to the pavilion of Caesaria. They went down three descents and up six. They came to the entrance of a beautiful cave. Inside was a prepared bed with lit oil lamps. Elijah held the head of Rabbi Akiva, and Rabbi Yehoshua held the feet. Together, they placed Rabbi Akiva on the bed.

For three days and three nights the ministering angels cried. Elijah and Rabbi Yehoshua then buried Rabbi Akiva in the cave. The following morning, Elijah accompanied the soul of Rabbi Akiva to the heavens. The souls of the righteous and honorable gathered to listen to Rabbi Akiva expound upon the letters of the Torah.

It was said of Rabbi Chananiah ben Tradion that he never wished another man ill. When the emperor decreed that Torah no longer be taught, Rabbi Chananiah ben Tradion assembled great masses in the open streets of Rome, held the Torah in his lap, and expounded on the Torah. The emperor ordered that the sage be wrapped in a Torah scroll and burned alive. The executioner wrapped Rabbi Chananiah ben Tradion in a scroll and placed wads of damp wool between the scroll and the rabbi's heart to make the suffering greater.

Rabbi Chananiah ben Tradion's daughter, who was made to watch, cried out, "Woe is to me to have to see my father suffer so."[6]

Rabbi Chananiah ben Tradion told her, "It is better for me to see this."

His students asked their teacher what he could see.

"I see parchment burning, but the letters are flying around," he said and began to cry.

His students asked why he was crying. "It would not be

so terrible if they burned only me, but they burn the Torah with me."

The executioner was moved by pity and asked the rabbi if he wished the wads of wool to be removed so that he would be able to go to his reward faster. The rabbi asked the executioner to remove the wool and fan the fires. The executioner did so and threw himself into the burning flames saying, "Rabbi, bring me with you into the World to Come."

A Heavenly Voice went out, "Some men serve the Lord their whole life and lose their reward in the last moment. Some men sin their whole life and gain reward the last moment."[7]

Rabbi Yehudah ben Bava had never slept a full night's sleep from the time he was eighteen until the day he died at age eighty.[8] He had taught his students day and night and addressed each one as "my teacher."

One of Rabbi Yehudah ben Bava's students, Rabbi Reuven ben Astrobul, asked that he take the place of his teacher for the execution.

The teacher replied, "It is a decree from above and cannot be abolished. Hold your words and recite the blessing 'The Judge of the Truth.'"

On Friday afternoon, Rabbi Yehudah ben Bava was brought by a Roman official to be executed. He begged the official to wait a few moments, for there was one more *mitzvah* he wished to do, reciting the *Shabbos Kiddush*.

"Do you still believe in your Lord?" the official wondered. "Does He still have powers?"

"The Lord is great and most praiseworthy," Rabbi

Yehudah ben Bava answered, "and there is no fathoming his greatness."

"Why doesn't He save you and your colleagues?" the official asked.

"We owe our lives to Him. He has given us into the hands of the evil emperor to do the work, so He may seek revenge."

When the official heard these words, he reported the matter to the emperor. The emperor had Rabbi Yehudah ben Bava brought before him.

"Is it true you uttered those words?" he asked.

"It is true," Rabbi Yehudah ben Bava replied.

"Such insolence. Here you stand before death's door and you display such boldness?"

Rabbi Yehudah ben Bava answered, "Woe to you, evil one, the son of an evil one. The Holy Blessed One saw you burn His House and murder his noble and righteous ones. He allows His anger to burn within so He can rage later with a terrible revenge."

Rabbi Yehudah ben Bava's students wondered why the rabbi insulted the emperor rather than appease him with words of flattery so his life would be spared.

"Did you not learn that whoever flatters a wicked man, in the end, will fall before him?" Rabbi Yehudah ben Bava answered.

Rabbi Yehudah ben Bava asked the emperor if he would wait a few moments so he could sanctify the Sabbath which is from the World to Come.

"I shall let you do so for your Lord," answered the emperor.

Rabbi Yehudah ben Bava began to recite the *Kiddush* with a strong and sweet voice, astounding those in attendance. As he was reciting the last verse, "that was created by the Lord to do," the emperor ordered him to be executed.[9] Rabbi Yehudah ben Bava died while uttering the Name of the Lord.

A Heavenly voice called out, "Fortunate are you, Rabbi Yehudah ben Bava. You are likened to the angels, and your soul departed with the Lord's Name."

At the order of the emperor, the body of Rabbi Yehudah ben Bava was butchered and thrown to the dogs. There was no burial, no eulogy.

Rabbi Yehudah ben Dama was brought with his students to be executed on the eve of *Shavuos*.[10] He requested that he be allowed to wait until evening time, when he would be able to perform one last *mitzvah*, the *Kiddush* of *Shavuos*, the day we received the holy Torah. The emperor was astounded that Rabbi Yehudah ben Dama retained his faith in the Lord. The emperor inquired as to the benefit of the Torah.

"King David, may his soul rest in peace, has told us that great benefits lie in store in the future for those who fear the Lord," Rabbi Yehudah ben Dama answered.

"You Jews are the greatest fools in the world to believe in the afterworld," scoffed the emperor.

The rabbi responded in kind. "There are no fools in the world like you, who deny the living Lord. Woe to you, you will be shamed, degraded and embarrassed when you see us basking in the glory of the Lord, the Light of Life, while you reside in the lowermost depths."

FROM THE MIDRASH [163]

The emperor was enraged and ordered that the sage and his students be executed. He commanded that the hair of Rabbi Yehudah ben Dama's head be tied to the tail of a horse and be dragged through the streets of Rome. After this was done, the sage's holy body was butchered and left in the streets. Elijah came and brought the limbs to the cave near the river that flows outside of Rome.

For the next thirty days, the Romans could hear the sounds of wailing and crying emanating from the cave. This was reported to the emperor, and he defiantly rebuked the Romans, "Even should the universe return to emptiness and void, I shall not cease until ten of them are slain as I have sworn."

One of the elderly wise men of Rome approached the emperor. "It is a mistake to do so. In the end, you shall regret what you have done. I have seen the Torah of the Jews, and it says that their Lord is long suffering, but eventually, He destroys His enemies with a vengeance."

The emperor was deeply annoyed at this elder and ordered that he be hanged. Before the wise man was killed, he circumcised himself and joined the flock of those who were to be sacrificed as an offering to the Lord. The elder was hanged, and suddenly, his body was gone, nowhere to be found. The emperor trembled with fright, but still his anger at the Jews raged and his hand was still stretched out against them.

Chutzpis the Interpreter was one hundred and thirty years old at the time he was killed. Though advanced in age, he still had the countenance of an angel. The Romans told the emperor of the rabbi's years and countenance and thought that perhaps the emperor would have pity on him. The sage was brought before the emperor.

"Old man, how old are you?"

"Tomorrow I will be one hundred and thirty. If it pleases the emperor, allow me to finish out this day and kill me the next."

"What difference does it make to you if you die today or tomorrow?" the emperor asked.

"I will be able to recite the *Shema* this evening and tomorrow morning and proclaim the majesty of the Lord's great and fearful name," was the reply.

The emperor yelled at Chutzpis the Interpreter, "How dare you insult me that way? I am the majesty. Your Lord cannot save you. My fathers have destroyed His House. The carcasses of the Jews were strewn around Jerusalem without being buried. Your Lord is too old to be of help any longer. Otherwise, He would rise up and take revenge as He did in times of old against Pharaoh, Sisera and the kings of Canaan."

When Chutzpis the Interpreter heard the emperor blaspheme the Name of the Lord, he tore his clothing and said, "Woe to you when the Lord avenges His great Name. Woe to you and your gods."

The emperor turned to those assembled. "Why do I continue to debate this old man? Stone him, and have his corpse hung up."

Out of respect for the great age of Chutzpis the Interpreter, the emperor allowed his students to bury him.

Rabbi Chananiah ben Chakinai had fasted all his days, from the time he was twelve years old until the day he was killed. His death came on the Sabbath Eve. His students asked if he wished to eat or drink before his death.

"My whole life, I never tasted anything during the day," he replied. "Now that I am about to die, why should I eat?"

He was executed while reciting the *Kiddush* of the Sabbath. He expired while saying the word "holy."

A Heavenly Voice issued forth, "Fortunate is Rabbi Chananiah ben Chakinai who was holy and died while saying 'holy.'"

Rabbi Yeshevav the Scribe was taken out on his ninetieth birthday.

His students asked him, "Rabbi, what will become of the Torah?"

"I see that the Torah is destined to be forgotten," Rabbi Yeshevav answered. "This cruel nation will use trickery and deceit to take the precious pearl from us. May my death be an atonement for such a fate."

"And what shall become of us?" the students asked.

"Strengthen yourselves with love and peace toward each other," replied Rabbi Yeshevav. "Then there shall be hope."

The emperor asked Rabbi Yeshevav the Scribe his age.

"Today I am ninety," he replied. "Before I left my mother's womb, it was already destined that my colleagues and I would be killed by your hand so that the Lord could avenge our blood."

"Do you believe in the World to Come?" the emperor then asked.

"Yes, and woe will be to you when His righteous ones are avenged." Rabbi Yeshevav the Scribe recited the *Shema* and as he recited the words, "And the Lord spoke to Moses, saying," the emperor gave an order to his guards.

"Quick, kill him," he called. "Let us see the strength and might of this Lord and what He will do in the next world."

Rabbi Yeshevav the Scribe was burned at the stake and the remains given to the dogs.[11]

Rabbi Elazar ben Shamua was killed on his one hundred and fifth birthday. It was also the day of *Yom Kippur*.[12] People said of Rabbi Elazar ben Shamua that a disparaging remark was never heard from his mouth. He never argued with his fellow man. He was renowned for his humility and quiet demeanor.

His students asked him what he saw.

"I see Rabbi Yehudah ben Bava and Rabbi Akiva discussing the law, and Rabbi Yishmael the High Priest decided the matter in favor of Rabbi Akiva. I also see the souls of the righteous immersing themselves in the Shiloach Brook to purify themselves so they may enter the heavenly academy and listen to the words of Rabbi Akiva ben Yosef in purity."

As soon as Rabbi Elazar ben Shamua said the word "purity," the emperor ordered his execution. A Heavenly voice called out, "Fortunate is Rabbi Elazar ben Shamua, for you are pure and your soul departed with 'purity.'"

NOTES

1. This chapter has been taken entirely from the *Midrash Asarah Harugei Malchus*, also called *Midrash Aileh Ezkerah*. There are four versions of the *Midrash* with some variations among them. The

midrash does vary on occasion from the Talmudic texts. Those differences are footnoted.

I) The following is the order of the Ten Martyrs as given in version 1 of the *Midrash*.

1. *Rabban Shimon ben Gamliel*
2. *Rabbi Yishmael*
3. *Rabbi Akiva*
4. *Rabbi Chananiah ben Tradion*
5. *Rabbi Yehudah ben Bava*
6. *Rabbi Yehudah ben Dama*
7. *Rabbi Chutzpis*
8. *Rabbi Chananiah ben Chakinai*
9. *Rabbi Yeshevav*
10. *Rabbi Elazar ben Shamua*

II) According to version 2:

1. *Rabban Shimon ben Gamliel*
2. *Rabbi Yishmael*
3. *Rabbi Akiva*
4. *Rabbi Yehudah ben Bava*
5. *Rabbi Chananiah ben Tradion*
6. *Rabbi Yeshevav*
7. *Rabbi Elazar ben Dama*
8. *Rabbi Chananiah ben Chakinai*
9. *Rabbi Chutzpis*
10. *Rabbi Elazar ben Shamua*

III) The *kinah* of *Tishah b'Av, Arzei Halevanon,* follows the order of *Midrash Aileh Ezkerah,* version 2, but deletes number (7) Rabbi Elazar ben Dama and (8) Rabbi Chananiah ben Chakinai.

IV) According to the *selichah* recited on *Erev Rosh Hashanah, Aileh Ezkerah,* the order is as follows:

1. *Rabban Shimon ben Gamliel*
2. *Rabbi Yishmael*
3. *Rabbi Akiva*

4. *Rabbi Chananiah ben Tradion*
5. *Rabbi Chutzpis*
6. *Rabbi Elazar ben Shamua*
7. *Rabbi Chananiah ben Chakinai*
8. *Rabbi Yeshevav*
9. *Rabbi Yehudah ben Dama*
10. *Rabbi Yehudah ben Bava*

V) According to the *Selichah* recited on *Erev Yom Kippur, El Elokim,* the order is as follows:

1. *Rabban Shimon ben Gamliel*
2. *Rabbi Yishmael*
3. *Rabbi Akiva*
4. *Rabbi Chananiah ben Tradion*
5. *Rabbi Chutzpis*
7. *Rabbi Chaninah ben Chakinai*
8. *Rabbi Yeshevav*
9. *Rabbi Yehudah ben Bava*
10. *Rabbi Yehudah ben Dama*

VI) The *Midrash* in *Eichah Rabah* (2:4) has an unusual list of the Ten Martyrs.

1. *Rabbi Yishmael*
2. *Rabban Gamliel*
3. *Rabbi Yeshevav*
4. *Rabbi Yehudah ben Bava*
5. *Rabbi Chutzpis*
6. *Rabbi Yehudah Hanachtum*
7. *Rabbi Chananiah ben Tradion*
8. *Rabbi Akiva*
9. *Ben Azzai*
10. *Rabbi Tarfon*

VII) Version 4 of the *Midrash Aileh Ezkerah* does not list the order of the Ten Martyrs, but it does the give the following list of names:

Rabbi Yishmael, Rabban Shimon ben Gamliel, Rabbi Elazar ben Dama, Rabbi Eliezer ben Shamua, Rabbi Eliezer ben Dahavoi, Chananiah ben Chakinai, Yonassan ben Uziel, Rabbi Akiva and Rabbi Yehudah ben Bava.

2. According to version 3, it was Rabbi Nechunia ben Hakanah who suggested to them that they ask for three day's time.

3. The *Midrash* gives the impression that the ten martyrs were killed at the same time. Actually, they were killed over a period of sixty-five years. The first ones, Rabban Shimon ben Gamliel and Rabbi Yishmael, were killed before the destruction of the Temple, in 70 C.E., and the rest were killed during the Hadrianic persecution, circa 135 C.E.

4. According to *Megillas Taanis, Maamar Acharon,* Rabban Shimon ben Gamliel and Rabbi Yishmael were killed on the twenty-fifth day of *Sivan*. It also states that Rabbi Chanina Segan Hakohanim was killed with them. He is not counted among the Ten Martyrs because only those who were comparable to the ten brothers of Joseph are given that appellation. The *Shalsheles Hakabalah* says that each of the ten martyrs corresponded to one of the ten brothers. Rabbi Yishmael, who was the High Priest from the tribe of Levi, corresponded to the brother Levi. Rabbi Chanina Segan Hakohanim was also from the tribe of Levi.

5. According to *Berachos* (60a), Rabbi Akiva died while saying the word "*echad*" in *Shema*.

6. Rabbi Chananiah ben Tradion had two daughters. This one and her mother were sold by the Romans to a house of ill repute. The other daughter, Beruriah, married Rabbi Meir. They fled to Babylonia. (*Avodah Zarah* 17, 18)

7. Version 2 records the strange story that somehow the emperor was switched with Rabbi Chananiah ben Tradion. The emperor was

killed and Rabbi Chananiah ruled for six months.

8. Version 2 states that Rabbi Yehudah ben Bava was seventy years of age.

9. According to the Talmud (*Sanhedrin* 14a), Rabbi Yehudah ben Bava was pierced by three hundred spears.

10. There is no mention of Rabbi Yehudah ben Dama in the Talmud. Version 2 says he was killed on account of his wearing *tefillin*.

11. Version 1 says Rabbi Yeshevav was burned alive. Version 2 says he was killed and thrown to the dogs.

12. Version 2 says Rabbi Elazar ben Shamua was killed reciting *Kiddush* on *Shabbos*.

13. According to the *kinah Arzei Halevanon*, he died by sword while reciting the *Kiddush*. He died with the words "which the Lord created" on his lips. Version 2 also mentions that Rabbi Elazar ben Shamua died while uttering the Lord's name in *Kiddush*.

THE MIDRASHIC ACCOUNT OF KAMTZA AND BAR KAMTZA

Our Sages placed great emphasis on the story of Kamtza and Bar Kamtza as symptomatic of the moral decay that led to the downfall of Jerusalem. "The destruction of Jerusalem came through Kamtza and Bar Kamtza." (*Gittin* 55b) The story of Kamtza and Bar Kamtza is recorded twice, once in the Talmud (*Gittin* 55b) and once in the *Midrash*. (*Eichah Rabah* 4:2-3)

This is the incident as recorded by the *Midrash*.

"The precious sons of Zion . . ." (*Lamentations* 4:2) What was their precious way? None would attend a feast unless he was invited twice. [This practice was developed to prevent one from attending a celebration to which one was mistakenly invited. (*Eitz Yosef*)]

An incident occurred with one [of the inhabitants of Jerusalem] who made a feast. He told a member of his household to go and bring Kamtza, his dear friend. [The member of the household] went and brought Bar Kamtza [the host's] enemy. [Bar Kamtza, the son of Kamtza, thought that the host invited him in order to honor his father, even though he was the enemy of the host. Or, he thought, perhaps he was invited in order to make peace between them. (*Eitz Chaim* quoting *Maharsha*)] [Bar Kamtza] entered and sat among the guests. [The host then] entered and found [Bar Kamtza] among those attending the feast.

[The host said:] "You are my enemy, and yet you sit in my house. Get up and leave my home."

[Bar Kamtza replied:] "Do not embarrass me. I shall pay for what I eat."

[The host said:] "You may not attend."

[Bar Kamtza replied:] "Do not embarrass me. I shall sit but not eat nor drink."

[The host insisted:] "You may not attend."

[Bar Kamtza offered:] "I am willing to pay the cost of the entire feast."

[The host was adamant.] "Get up [and leave]!"

Among the attendants was Rabbi Zechariah ben Avkulas. He had the authority to object [to the host's abuse], but he did not. [He did not wish to show his authority inside the home of another. (*Eitz Yosef*)]

[Bar Kamtza] went outside and said to himself, "They gather and sit in merriment. [They eat and drink, thinking they have nothing to fear. (*Eitz Yosef*)] I will go and inform [the Roman government] against them."

What did he do? He went to the [Roman] emperor and said, "The sacrifices that you send to the Jews to offer in the Temple, they eat it themselves and offer others in its stead."

[The emperor] rebuked [Bar Kamtza] and sent him away in disbelief. [Bar Kamtza later] returned and said [to the emperor] again, "All those sacrifices that you send to the Jews, they eat it themselves and offer others in their stead. If you do not believe me, send with me some sacrifices and one of your servants, and you will soon know if I am a liar."

One night, while they were on the way [to the Temple], the [emperor's] servant fell asleep, and Bar Kamtza arose and secretly made blemishes on all [the sacrifices]. When the [Temple] priest saw [the blemishes], he offered other [sacrifices] in their stead.

The royal servant asked, "Why did you not offer those sacrifices [that I had brought]?"

[The priest] said, "Tomorrow [I shall offer them]."

[The servant] came back on the third day [after leaving the emperor], but [the sacrifices] were not offered.

[The servant] sent word to the king, "The matter of which the Jew told you is true."

Immediately, [the emperor] rose up against the Temple, and [eventually] it was destroyed.

That is why people say, "Because of the difference between [the names] Kamtza and Bar Kamtza the Temple was destroyed." [The people thought that the destruction of the Temple was the fault of the careless member of the household of the host who had sent the wrong invitation. (*Eitz Yosef*)]

Rabbi Yossi said, "It was because of the tolerance of Rabbi Zechariah ben Avkulas [who refused to rebuke the abusive host] that the Sanctuary was burned."

This is the version of the incident as recorded in the *Midrash*. The incident was initially recorded to illustrate what happens when one attends a feast without having been invited twice. This would indicate that Bar Kamtza was to blame. At the end of the story, the dictum of the populace is quoted to show that they thought the blame rested with the one who mixed up the names Kamtza and Bar Kamtza. The *Midrash* ends with Rabbi Yossi placing the guilt at the feet of Rabbi Zechariah's tolerance of the host's abuse. Rabbi Yossi's statement is reiterated in the *Tosefta*. (*Shabbos* 17:4) Rabbi Yossi said, "The tolerance of Rabbi Zechariah ben Avkulas burned the Sanctuary."

This incident is also recorded in the Talmud. (*Gittin* 55b)

Rabbi Yochanan said, "What exemplifies the verse, 'Fortunate is the man who always fears, but he who hardens his heart shall fall into evil?' (*Mishlei* 28:14) The destruction of Jerusalem came through Kamtza and Bar Kamtza. A certain man had a dear friend Kamtza and an enemy Bar

Kamtza. He made a feast and said to his attendant, "Go and bring Kamtza to me." [The attendant] went and brought Bar Kamtza. [The host] came and found that [Bar Kamtza] was sitting [at his feast].

[The host said:] "Since you are my enemy, what are you doing here? Get up and leave."

[Bar Kamtza replied:] "Since I am already here, let me stay and I will pay for what I eat and drink."

[The host said:] "No!"

[Bar Kamtza said:] "I will pay you half the cost of the feast [if you allow me to stay]."

[The host refused:] "No!"

[Bar Kamtza persisted:] "I am willing to pay the cost of the entire feast."

[The host still refused:] "No!"

[The host] took [Bar Kamtza] by the hand, stood him up and threw him out.

[Bar Kamtza] said, "Since the rabbis attended and raised no objection, I can infer they condoned what occurred. I shall go and inform against them to the government."

[Bar Kamtza] went and told the emperor, "The Jews are rebelling against you."

[The emperor] replied, "Who says so?"

[Bar Kamtza] said, "Send them a sacrifice and see if they offer it."

[The emperor] sent a prime calf with [Bar Kamtza]. While on the way, [Bar Kamtza] made a blemish on the calf's upper lip; some say on the white of the eye. According to [Jewish Law] these constitute blemishes, but according to [pagan practices] these do not constitute blemishes. The rabbis were willing to offer [the sacrifice] to keep the peace with the government.

Rabbi Zechariah ben Avkulas said to them, "[People] will say blemished animals can be offered on the Altar."

[The rabbis] thought to kill [Bar Kamtza to prevent him from getting word back to the emperor that the sacrifice was rejected.] Rabbi Zechariah said to them, "[People] will say that [Bar Kamtza] was killed for making a blemish on a sacrifice [and surely you do not wish people to think that causing a blemish deserves such a severe penalty]."

Rabbi Yochanan said, "The tolerance of Rabbi Zechariah ben Avkulas caused the destruction of our House, the burning of the Sanctuary and the exile from our land." [Rabbi Zechariah should have exercised his authority and allowed the rabbis to kill Bar Kamtza. (Rashi)]

That is the version as recorded in the Talmud. The Talmud does not mention that Rabbi Zechariah was the rabbi who attended the feast. It does say that he was the rabbi who rejected Emperor Nero's sacrifice. Rabbi Yochanan, in the Talmud, blames Rabbi Zechariah's refusal to have Bar Kamtza killed as the cause for the Temple's destruction. The *Midrash* does not mention that it was Rabbi Zechariah who refused to accept the sacrifice. It does say that Rabbi Zechariah was the rabbi who attended the feast. Rabbi Yossi blames Rabbi Zechariah's condoning silence at the feast as the cause for the Temple's eventual destruction. Both Rabbi Yochanan and Rabbi Yossi attributed the blame to Rabbi Zechariah's inaction; they merely disagree as to which inaction was the primary cause. Possibly, Rabbi Yossi agrees with Rabbi Yochanan that the later inaction was the more severe. However, Rabbi Yossi thought that had Rabbi Zechariah spoken out at the feast and rebuked the host, the later part of the incident would not have occurred. Therefore, Rabbi Yossi recorded the first incident as the primary cause.

Rabbi Zechariah ben Avkulas was a great sage. His view on a matter concerning one of the laws of the Sabbath is recorded in the Talmud (*Shabbos* 143a), and his opinion is recorded in the Code of Law (*Shulchan Aruch, Orach Chaim* 308:30) as the proper conduct of a "great man." His greatness was his "tolerance." The Hebrew term employed in the Talmud, *Tosefta* and *Midrash* regarding Rabbi Zechariah's tolerance is *anvesanusa*. The root of the word is *anav*, humble. It was because of Rabbi Zechariah's humble demeanor that he declined to speak up at the feast against the host. It was his humble demeanor that did not allow him to have Bar Kamtza killed. In the end, it was this humility in front of the abusive host, this tolerance before the vengeful Bar Kamtza, that allowed him to remain silent. Silence in the face of injustice destroyed the Temple.

Glossary of
Historical Places and Persons

Amigdolin Pool: Today it is called Chizkiyahu's Pool. This was a cistern used to supply the Tower of David fortress with water. The name Amigdolin comes from the Hebrew word *migdal*, tower. The remains of this cistern can be seen from the Tower of David. The pool is located about one hundred and fifty feet to the southwest of the tower.

Antiochus Epiphanes: King of Commagene in Syria in the First Century c.e., not to be confused with the infamous Antiochus in the story of *Chanukah*, who lived two hundred years earlier.

Antonia Fortress: One of two fortresses in Jerusalem. The other was the Tower of David. The Antonia was originally built by the Hasmoneans and was called Baris or Birah. It was rebuilt by King Herod and named after Mark Anthony. It occupied the northern section of the Temple Mount. It is referred to in the Jerusalem Talmud. The only remains that exist today are a few flooring stones.

Assyrian Camp: This site is located in today's Morashah district in the New City, near the intersection of Haneviim and Shivtei Yisrael Streets. Some archaeologists believe it is located outside Meah Shearim in the "Russian Compound."

Commagene: A district in Syria.

Ein Gedi: An oasis town about ten miles north of Masada.

Fortress of David: See Tower of David.

Gush Chalav: A small town five miles north of Safed. The remains of a second century synagogue can still be seen there.

Hebron: A very ancient city south of Jerusalem. The Mearas Hamachpeilah is located there. The structure over the cave was built by King Herod, and its outer walls are similar to the Temple walls as they would have appeared two thousand years ago. This structure and its walls, however, were built on a much smaller scale than the Temple.

Helena: Queen of Adiabene, a province in Mesopotamia. The entire royal family converted to Judaism. During the time of Hillel, she moved to Jerusalem and lived south of the Temple in the Lower City. The royal tombs, built for her family, were one of the architectural marvels of ancient

Jerusalem. Their remains are located in the Sheik Jarrah district of the New City. They are called Tomb of the Kings. Helena is referred to several times in the Talmud.

Hinnom Valley: To the west of the Temple Mount was the Western Hill. It was bounded on the east by the Tyropean Valley, which separated the Western Hill from the Temple Mount, and on the west by the Valley of Hinnom. The Hinnom Valley went from north to south where it joined with the Kidron Valley. In ancient times, the fire-god Molech was worshipped there. In later times, the valley served as a trash heap where the refuse of the city was burned. The constant fires and wretched stench served as a visual image for the nether world.

Herod: King of Judea one hundred years before the destruction. Known as a great builder, he enlarged and rebuilt the Holy Temple. The Temple walls that remain today, including the Western Wall, were built by Herod. Much of Josephus' writings are concerned with the reign of this maniacal and despotic tyrant.

Herod, Monuments of: Some ruins can be found on a grassy knoll to the north of the Damascus Gate of the Old City. Possibly, these are the remains of the Herodian monuments.

Herodian Palace: The Palace of Herod was to the south of the Tower of David. Some remains of the palace foundation can be seen in the present day Tower of David.

Hippicus Tower: One of the three towers that stood in the Tower of David. It was built by Herod and named after his friend who was killed in battle. Remains of the Herodian towers in the Tower of David can still be seen.

Kidron Valley: The valley between the Temple Mount and the Mount of Olives. It curves to the west about a half mile below the Temple Mount, where it meets the Hinnom Valley. From there, the Kidron goes south to the Dead Sea.

Lower City: The Temple was built on top of a mountain called Mount Moriah. To the west was another mountain, called the Western Hill or the Upper City. Between the two mountains was the Tyropean Valley. The present day Old City is built atop the Western Hill. The homes and estates constructed in the Upper City comprised the aristocratic section of ancient Jerusalem. Here the noblemen, High Priests and other aristocrats lived. The Royal Palace was at the very top of the Upper City next to the Fortress of David. The site of the palace is occupied today by a police station and an Armenian church. The district in ancient Jerusalem that was built on the southern slope of the eastern mountain, Mount Moriah, was called the Lower City. The eastern section of the Lower City was called the Ophel.

Masada: A fortress in the Judean Desert, built by Herod.

Mount of Olives: The mountain to the east of the Temple Mount. It has two peaks. The higher one, to the north, is today occupied by a church. The lower peak, to the south, is occupied by the Intercontinental Hotel.

Mount Scopus: A mountain northeast of the Temple Mount, occupied today by the Hebrew University. Several ancient tombs are found there.

Place of Trumpeting: A plaque referring to "the Place of the Trumpeting" was discovered in the debris southwest of the Temple Mount.

Psephinus Tower: The largest tower of the ancient city, no remains of which have been found. It was located in the present day Meah Shearim district, near the corner of Devorah Haneviah and Haneviim Streets.

Serpent's Pool: Probably identified with the present day Mamilla Pool. It is the largest of the ancient cisterns still in existence. It is located in Independence Park behind the Sheraton Plaza Hotel. One of the primary sources of water in the ancient city was the Gichon (Gihon). It would appear that the Gichon was a system of aqueducts that snaked their way from the springs in the Judean Desert into Jerusalem; *gichon* is Hebrew for "snake." Some of the water brought in by the aqueduct was stored in the Serpent's Pool. Parts of the aqueduct system, some dating back to the First Temple era, are still in existence.

Shimon ben Gamliel: Rabban Shimon ben Gamliel the Elder, one of the "ten martyrs" killed in 70 c.e. See Yishmael.

Sicarikon: A radical band of Zealot outlaws founded by Abba Sicarika, circa 50 c.e. The Talmud (*Gittin* 56a) refers to a radical group called the Biryonim or Baryonim. If the word is Biryonim, it could be derived from *biron*, meaning the palace or elite guard. If the term is Baryonim, it may be derived from *baryos*, meaning rebel or revolutionary. The distinction between Sicarikon and Biryonim is unclear.

Shiloach Brook: A naturally flowing river in Jerusalem, located to the south of the ancient city. Many archeological writings concern themselves with the site of the river and identify it with the so-called Tunnel of Chizkiyahu, but this seems unlikely. Chizkiyahu diverted the Gichon and not the Shiloach. See Serpent's Pool.

Tiberius Alexander: The son of a pious and generous Jew, Tiberius Alexander converted to paganism and became a viceroy in Egypt. He later became a Roman military leader participating in the destruction of the Holy City.

Tower of David: From the time of King David, fortresses were constructed at this site, near the present day Jaffa Gate. Its purpose was to protect the western side of the city, Jerusalem's most vulnerable point. The ruins of many of the fortresses can be seen at the site today.

Tyropean Valley: The valley that separated the Temple Mount from the Western Hill. In ancient times, the Western Hill was known as the Upper City. Today, the Western Hill is called the Old City. The plaza in front of the Western

Wall is located in the Tyropean Valley. Its original base was forty feet below where one stands at the Western Wall today.

Upper City: See Lower City.

Women's Courtyard: The Temple consisted of several concentric courtyards. The innermost courtyard, called the *Azarah*, was the most sacred. To the east of the *Azarah* was the Women's Courtyard. Here, the ceremony of the Drawing of the Water was celebrated on *Sukkos*. The women watched from the galleries above, while the men danced below.

Women's Gate: The northern gate of the ancient city, located to the south of the Tomb of Kings (see Helena) on St. George Street. No remains have yet been found.

Yishmael, the High Priest: Rabbi Yishmael ben Elisha, one of the "ten martyrs" immortalized in the *kinos* and in the *Mussaf* service for *Yom Kippur* in *Aileh Ezkerah*, "There shall I remember."

Yochanan the High Priest: Also known as Hyrcanus, a Hasmonean king. Lived 175 b.c.e. until 104 b.c.e. His burial vault is located behind the King David Hotel. It is mistakenly called Herod's Family Tomb.

GLOSSARY

Amoraim: Torah scholars mentioned in the *Gemara*

Chanukah: Festival of Lights

erev: the eve of

galus: exile

halachah (halachos): Jewish laws

Kiddush: sanctification of *Shabbos* or Festivals

Kinos: Lamentations

maaser: tithe

matzoh (matzos): unleavened bread(s)

menorah: candelabra

Midrash: body of homiletics from Talmudic period

mikveh: ritual bath

Mishnah: part of the Talmud

mitzvah (mitzvos): Torah commandment(s)

Mussaf: supplementary service

Shavuos: Pentecost, late spring festival

shekel: coin

Shema Yisrael: Hear, O Israel

shofar: ram's horn

Shulchan Aruch: Code of Jewish Law

Sukkos: Festival of Tabernacles, autumn festival

tallis: prayer shawls

tefillin: phylacteries

Tishah b'Av: the Ninth of Av, a fast day

yeshivah: Torah schools

Yom Kippur: Day of Atonement